ARIE
2025
(Annual Horoscope 2025)

Dr Gautam DK
Naresh Gautam

First Edition June 2024

Copyright © 2024 Gautam DK

Request for permission should be addressed to Dr Gautam DK at astrogautamdk@gmail.com

Prayer

|| om gaṁ gaṇapataye namaḥ ||

|| brahmā murāristripurāntakārī bhānuḥ śaśī bhūmisuto budhaśca guruśca śukraḥ śanirāhuketavaḥ sarve grahāḥ śānti karā bhavantu ||

Brahmā (the Creator), Murāri (Vishnu, the Sustainer), Tripurāntakarin (Śiva, the slayer of the demon Tripurāsura), Bhānu (the Sun), Shashin (the Moon), Bhūmisuta (Mars, the son of the Earth), Budha (Mercury), Guru (Jupiter), Shukra (Venus), Shani (Saturn), Rāhu and Ketu, may all these Grahas be peaceful.

Books by the Author

General Series

1. *Marriage Astrology*
2. *Matchmaking for Marriage*
3. *Love Marriage*
4. *Mangal Dosha*
5. *Lal Kitab*
6. *Astrology for Beginners- Twelve Houses of Chart Vol I*
7. *Astrology for Beginners – Planets in Astrology Vol II*
8. *Astrology for Beginners – 12 Zodiac Signs Vol III*
9. *Ashwini Nakshatra*
10. *Bharani Nakshatra*
11. *World of Souls*

Planet Series

1. *Rahu Nature and Behaviour*
2. *Rahu in Twelve Houses of Chart*
3. *Rahu in Twelve Houses of Chart (Hindi)*
4. *Ketu in Twelve Houses of Chart*
5. *Mercury in Astrology*
6. *Jupiter in Twelve Houses of Chart*
7. *Saturn in Twelve Houses of Chart*

Annual Horoscope 2024 Series

1. *Aries Horoscope 2024*
2. *Gemini Horoscope 2024*
3. *Cancer Horoscope 2024*
4. *Leo Horoscope 2024*
5. *Virgo Horoscope 2024*
6. *Libra Horoscope 2024*
7. *Sagittarius Horoscope 2024*
8. *Capricorn Horoscope 2024*

9. *Aquarius Horoscope 2024*

10. *Pisces Horoscope 2024*

11. *Rahu Ketu Transit 2023-2025*

Annual Horoscope 2025 Series

1. *Aries Horoscope 2025*

2. *Taurus Horoscope 2025*

3. *Gemini Horoscope 2025*

4. *Cancer Horoscope 2025*

5. *Leo Horoscope 2025*

6. *Virgo Horoscope 2025*

7. *Libra Horoscope 2025*

8. *Scorpio Horoscope 2025*

9. *Sagittarius Horoscope 2025*

10. *Capricorn Horoscope 2025*

11. *Aquarius Horoscope 2025*

12. *Pisces Horoscope 2025*

Introduction

As we bid farewell to 2024 and greet the New Year 2025, we embrace the hope that comes with new beginnings. Time is in constant flux, and the future remains a mystery, offering both trials and opportunities. The cycle of time keeps moving, ushering in fresh experiences and transformations.

In the year 2025, hope shines as we continue to recover from the aftermath of the major ups and downs that have impacted businesses, markets, and health worldwide. The ongoing conflicts in Ukraine, Israel – Ghaza etc persisting for a long time add to the complexities of the global situation. Moreover, the pressing concern of global warming is disrupting our natural weather patterns, leading to more frequent cyclones and unexpected floods. Nature's expression through extreme weather events reminds us of the importance of sustainable development and environmental conservation.

Let's explore the significance of the coming year, 2025, based on your Zodiac Sign. Each sign experiences unique outcomes in the upcoming year. What does your Zodiac Sign have in store for you in 2025? What changes will it bring into our lives and what can we expect in social, political, and others? What lies ahead for you regarding education, love, marriage, children, career, potential career changes, job promotions, business expansion, financial prospects, clearance of debt, health, property matters, travel to foreign lands, social network and new ventures?

I want to cover this annual horoscope in six chapters. In the first chapter, we will cover the transit of planets in the year 2025 and its implications at mundane level. How the movement of planets is going to affect the world on various fronts at the geopolitics, politics, economy, finances, food production, tourism and healthcare. In the second chapter, we will cover the important dates during which major events at the mundane level will happen. These two chapters will be common for the annual horoscope 2025 series.

In the third chapter, we will cover the basic characteristics of a particular zodiac sign. In the fourth chapter, we will cover the Year 2025 for that zodiac sign. It will be based on the transit of major planets and conjunctions affecting for a longer duration. In this chapter, we will be covering the Year 2025 predictions in terms of general, profession, finances, health, love life and marriage, progeny, education and spiritualism

In the fifth chapter, we will go through month-wise predictions for the zodiac sign. These predictions will be primarily based upon the transit of the Sun and then the effect of other planets. This will be precise to plan the activity for each month.

In the sixth chapter, we go through the particular dates of each month in the year 2025 and likely effect on the zodiac sign. This will cover the results at two-day span level as it will be based on the movement of Moon in various signs. In the second part of this chapter, we will be covering the predictions on daily basis. This will be based on the movement of Moon over various Nakshatras. This will help to plan the day-to-day activity for the entire year. In the next chapter, we will cover the Sade Sati effects on Aries sign and recommend a few remedies that will help to mitigate the negative effects of Shani.

From Aries to Pisces, each sign will experience different opportunities and challenges, tailored to their personality traits. Get ready for the ups and downs of life as we reveal what the stars have in store for you.

Astrology is an ancient art and science that has guided humanity for centuries. It provides a deeper understanding of ourselves and the world. Our goal is to empower you with knowledge, helping you make informed decisions and avail the opportunities in 2025.

Events in a person's life are indeed influenced by the positions of planets in their birth chart. The timing of these events is determined by the planetary periods (Dasha and Antar Dasha), and the planetary transits indicate when the results of those events will manifest. **If an event is not promised in the birth chart and is not aligned with the current planetary periods, the transits might not have a significant impact.**

The concept of Desh (place), Kaal (time), and Patar (individual) plays a crucial role in shaping the outcomes of astrological influences. Results can vary based on geographical location, time, and the individual's unique circumstances. In our Zodiac, there are twelve zodiac signs, and each sign represents about 1/12th of the world's population. However, it's impractical to think that the predictions based on these signs will apply perfectly to everyone. They cannot be applied to every person with the same zodiac sign. What might be a fortunate time for a wealthy person could translate differently for someone with fewer resources. Even individuals born at the same time (like twins) can experience different life paths due to the interplay of their choices and actions (karma) alongside astrological influences.

Destiny is a complex interplay of cosmic influences, personal choices, and life circumstances. It's a dynamic interaction that can guide, but not completely dictate, the course of one's life. While the stars influence us, remember, it's our own choices (free will) that shape our destiny. Keep in mind that the future isn't fixed, and our decisions create our reality.

As a disclaimer, I would like to mention that the future is unpredictable and even our Rishis during Ramayana times could not predict the future of Maa Sita or Lord Ram. We can only try to predict events based on planetary movements, which is derived from knowledge from scriptures and experience. No one in the world can give assurance that an event will happen and with what intensity. We, astrologers, try to decipher with the best of our capabilities and intentions so that we can guide mankind to prepare themselves for any eventuality.

These predictions are general and offer some caution, warnings, and indications based on the movements of major planets like Saturn, Jupiter, Rahu, and Ketu. Individual predictions depend on the specific positions of planets at the time of a person's birth. For better clarity, it is recommended to consult an astrologer. You should consider this a general guide to make preparations before making major decisions. While astrology can provide insights and guidance, it's important to remember that there might not be remedies for certain fixed or incurable karmic situations, as these are aspects of life that individuals may need to face. Everyone has to burn his karmas to progress further in their metaphysical world.

Let's welcome the transformative energies of 2025 and make it a year of growth, joy, and self-discovery. May this book be your guiding light, leading you to your dreams. We wish you a year filled with cosmic blessings and endless possibilities!

****

2025: Astrological Overview

Based on the position and movement of planets in the year 2025, we need to decipher how it is going to affect the world on various fronts as world economy, politics, finances, food production, tourism and healthcare.

The planetary position as of 01 Jan 2025 at 00.01 hrs will be as under:

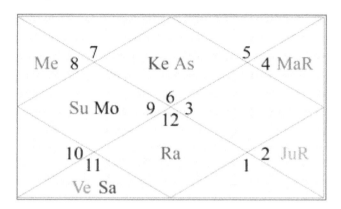

We will go through the transit of planets in the period 01 Jan 2025 to 31 Dec 2025 and try to decipher their implications. We consider the Kaal Purush Kundli (natural horoscope) for the world events.

Jupiter in transit in the Taurus sign, is retrograde on 09 Oct 2024 and will be direct on 4 Feb 2025. Jupiter enters Gemini sign on 14 May 2025 and Cancer sign on 18 Oct 2025. Jupiter becomes retrograde for 119 days on 11 Nov 2025 and re-enters Gemini sign on 05 Dec 2025. Apart from this, it will remain combust from 22 June to 16 July 2025. During the combustion period, there are no auspicious activities or functions planned.

Saturn is in transit in the Aquarius sign in the year 2023. It will transit to Pisces sign on 29 Mar 2025. Saturn goes for retrogradation from 13 July 2025 to 28 Nov 2025 for a period of 139 days. With Saturn transit in Aquarius since 2023, Sade Sati is going on for Pisces, Aquarius and Capricorn signs. These three signs are facing a lot of problems and obstacles in their life due to Saturn's Sade Sati effect. Saturn will transit to Pisces on 29 Mar 2025 and with this the Sade Sati of Capricorn will be over but Sade Sati for Aries will begin.

During this period, Mars will be retrograde in Cancer from 7 Dec 2024 and re-enter in Gemini sign on 21 Jan 2025. Mars becomes direct on 24 Feb 2025 and transit to Cancer sign on 3 Apr 2025, Leo on 7 June 2025, Virgo on 28 Jul 2025, Scorpio on 27 Oct 2025, and Sagittarius on 7 Dec 2025.

Details of Venus and Mercury transit are given at the end of the book.

Venus will be retrograde from 2 Mar to 13 Apr 2025. I find that Venus's signs Libra and Taurus will remain free from any major afflictions of Saturn, Rahu and Ketu in 2025. Something to celebrate for people of these signs. On 25 Mar 2025, Saturn will transit to Pisces and aspect the Taurus sign.

Mercury will be retrograde from 15 Mar to 07 Apr 205 in Pisces, 18 July to 11 Aug 2025 in Cancer,10 Nov to 29 Nov 2025 with transit from Scorpio to Libra on 23 Nov 2025.

Mercury generally retrogrades for the period of 20 to 24 days. During the retrogradation of Mercury, there may be a reversal in actions and speech, indicating shifts in speech abilities, communication skills, and decision-making abilities. People will tend to display either highly introverted or highly extroverted behavior. They may tend to express themselves excessively or may struggle to express themselves at all. At times, they can make unpredictable decisions or sudden decisions that surprise others. Period 15 Mar to 07 Apr 2025, when Mercury conjuncts with Rahu and later on 18 Mar 2025, Saturn Joins, the period will be quite challenging as the decisions made during this period may be disastrous.

In the year 2025, there will be two lunar (13-14 Mar 2025, 07-08 Sep 2025) and two solar (29 Mar 2025, 21 Sep 2025) eclipses. Details are given at the end of the book. These eclipses assume importance and can cause various unpleasant events in the world. You may observe incidents within 20-30 days of their occurrence.

Geopolitics

Countries and political parties will make new alliances. You will find major shifts in existing alliances as enemies of one time may become friends. I find India's relations with Western countries further improving after June 2024. Even after 14 May 2025, once Jupiter moves to Gemini, India continue to grow as a more responsible and powerful country. Other countries may look to India for guidance and help and India emerge as stronger. India will be treated as Vishwaguru, or a guide or someone who can resolve conflicts between the countries. India may initiate talks with Pakistan or will provide some relief during its crisis.

You may notice that during this period, the religious conversion issue will be in focus. Till 18 May 2025, Rahu in Jupiter house is indicative of large-scale conversions to the religious belief system. This may be by force luring them with money or indoctrination by their religious leaders. fundamentalists will try to hijack the agenda and dominate the government and the public. Demand for a separate homeland or to implement laws based on religion will increase causing protests in several countries. Religious fundamentalism will rise further and start disturbing the law and order of many countries.

After 18 May 2025, few countries or religious lobbies may ally to counter the religious fundamentalist forces. There may be a further rise of ISIS or any new organisation or some Christians may rise against Muslim fundamentalism. Few countries may look seriously at the refugee issue and may take some strong action. Governments will try to control the religious conversion momentum.

During the period Mar 2025 to July 2025, one solar and one lunar eclipse are being observed apart from Kaal Sarp Yoga. It creates a war-like situation between different countries. War may or may not happen but weapon industry lobbies will try to create a situation when countries will increase purchases of weapons and material of destruction.

In my annual horoscope for 2024, I have already predicted that The situation may aggravate further resulting in the involvement of more countries in this war. The war is going to be between two different religious ideologies which may have devastating effects. Collateral damage in Ghaza is likely to create a new breeding ground for terrorism and feed terrorist organisations like

Hamas. Muslim population worldwide is going to create a wave of sympathisers and more countries will get entangled in this. Struggle between Muslim and non-Muslim populations may create a major rift. If the issues are not resolved then you will find a greater number of countries will get involved in this creating a situation of world War and the most probable period is when Rahu and Saturn conjunct in Mar to May 2025.

The collateral damages in Ghaza have given a forum to various groups all over the US, UK and EU countries where they are putting pressure on Govt to cut ties with Israel. Initially, govt ignored those protests but now governments are using force to control those protests. Settlement of Palestine refugees also becomes a major issue. Iran also fired at Israel and the UN is trying to put pressure on Israel to stop the war. Though Israel will be completing its offensive in Ghaza liberation of Ghaza from Israel will be an issue of discord which will become a reason for instability in the entire region. There is the possibility of more and more countries getting involved in this turmoil. The situation will be critical during the period Mar to May 2025.

European Union will pass through a difficult phase of staying together as there will be a lot of discontentment and disagreement. The war between Ukraine and Russia may become nonrelevant as Ukraine finally agrees not to join NATO.

India's relationship with the US may be stressed as both countries for their national interests and under pressure from the media may have conflict issues.

Politics

Saturn's position in Aquarius, its Mool-trikona Sign, holds great significance, particularly in areas related to career, government, politics, and foreign affairs. However, there may be ups and downs in political issues from July to November 2025, due to Saturn's retrograde motion. Political parties will develop new strategies and try to destabilize existing elected governments worldwide. Misuse of deep fake videos using AI for propaganda will emerge as another battleground.

Finances and Wealth

Stock markets will continue to grow in the year 2025, as Jupiter is progressing towards the Cancer sign, which is a sign of its exaltation. There will be a surge in economic activities. All sectors will boom and give good results. Jupiter gets exalted in the Cancer sign and as it moves towards its exaltation sign, the financial sector booms. Stock markets and Gold will give good results.

Correction in the stock market will be observed after 11 Nov 2025, when Jupiter becomes retrograde. This correction may be for the duration of five to six months. Then markets will again rebound to new levels. This upward trend may continue till Dec 2026. Thereafter I find the markets will be looking for a correction. Prices of Gold and even property may also rise during the same time frame and thereafter look for correction. That correction may not be instant but at a gradual pace.

The year 2025 will provide much relief to everyone. The economic sector will grow, providing more and more employment opportunities of job. However, the Jobs will be skilled or knowledge-based industry rather than semiskilled. Artificial intelligence will continue to replace the human workforce. Those who upgrade themselves will be able to survive otherwise will perish. The world will continue to depend on unskilled labour, but the demand for the same will continue to fall.

The property market will escalate after May 2025, as Saturn will transit in Pisces and this trend will continue for the next 2.5 years. There may be some correction during the retrograde periods of Jupiter and Saturn.

Tourism

Rahu in the Aquarius sign after 18 May 2025, is quite indicative of increased trends in travels to foreign countries. The trend to visit foreign countries will increase. The business of travel agents and tour operators will outgrow. The travel agencies and tour operators will make a lot of money. However, the public will be looking for countries having cheaper cost of living.

Food Production

Rahu transit in Pisces till 18 May 2025, the exaltation sign of Venus indicates an increase in means to enjoyment. Life standards of people will improve as more consumer products will penetrate the markets. On 25 Mar 2025, Saturn will transit to Pisces and aspect Taurus, sign of Venus. Taurus is a sign of the entertainment and food industry. Jupiter presence in Taurus from 01 May 2024 to 18 May 2025 indicates that the entertainment and hospitality business will boom. They may adopt new means to reach the masses, especially after the Artificial intelligence and chat GPT. New platforms will emerge to replace the old systems. All the creator needs to upgrade themselves to meet the technology challenges. This advice applies to all people involved in the entertainment industry and hospitality business.

In 2025, there will be bumper production of food grains as Jupiter will expand the reservoirs of food grains. Technology such as the usage of Drones and genetically modified seeds will enhance food production. The commodity market will get a boost.

However, the production of crops after May 2025 will drop. There may be famine or critical food shortage in a few countries. But the world has become one at the commodity level so famine in one place does not mean much scarcity of food, provided you have money.

Healthcare

Healthcare systems may witness a crash during the period Mar to July 2025 as new bacteria or viruses affecting the digestive system may come up. This disease will affect the stomach and digestion-related issues. The reason may lie in polluted water and air. A lot of people in healthcare will be infected due to this disease. One of the reasons for the spread of the same may be contaminated and infected water or air. The healthcare industry will make a fortune out of this disease. The situation will affect a large population in the world.

Disasters

After 29 Mar 2025, Saturn will transit to Pisces, the sign of Jupiter. Pisces is the last zodiac sign, indicating detachment, transformation, expenditure and losses. Saturn placement is not good in the Pisces sign. During Saturn transit in the water sign, you may find cases or increases in hurricanes, cyclones, earthquakes, oil spills, pollution of water, nuclear leakages, pollution of water bodies, deficient rainfall etc.

Events During the Periods

12 Feb to 14 Apr 2025

Sun conjunct with Saturn in Aquarius sign from 12 Feb to 14 Mar 2025. Sun is in transit over Saturn indicating the state of disagreement between the public and government. There may be a lot of unrest, agitations and law and order problems. Death of any senior renowned politician can happen during this time. The government may try to implement some orders which are not acceptable to a few sections of society. Resulting unrest.

Rahu Sun conjunct in Pisces sign from 14 Mar to 14 Apr 2025. Saturn joins the conjunction on 29 Mar 2025. Rahu can corrupt the government authorities and they can use their powers arbitrarily without any justifications. Sun Rahu or Mars Rahu conjunction indicates fires, accidents or heat waves. In March – April 2025, again some major tragedy will take place which may be related to water and heat. Terrorist activities or riot-like situations cannot be overruled during this period.

Major Alert: 29 Mar to 29 July 2025

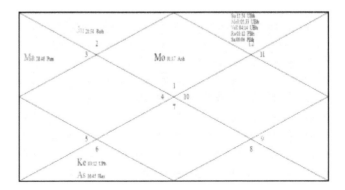

Saturn transit in Pisces on 29 Mar 2025 and conjunct with Rahu till 18 May 2025. This period may be one of the worst, as, during April 2025, Sun, Mercury and Venus will be under the effect of Rahu and Saturn. Mars will be in debilitation and that indicates a major problem at the Mundane level. During this period, there may be a major loss of lives, property and human rights due to war between countries, diseases or terrorist action. You may notice that Kaal Sarp Yoga is being formed from 29 Mar 2025 to 29 July 2025. This may be the time when terrorist organisations attack Western countries. Presently, Israel is in the process of finishing the Hamas, a terrorist wing of Palestine. In the process and excessive use of force, there will be a lot of collateral damage. Remember collateral damage creates more enmity and the resultant force emerging is more lethal, evolved and dangerous. Those forces may try to cause a lot of instability worldwide.

If we go down history, the similar planetary position of Kaal Sarp Yoga was formed from June to Sep 2005. Several unpleasant events happened during that period. On 07 July 2005, four coordinated suicide bombings hit central London, killing 52 people and injuring over 700. On 23 July 2005, a series of bombings hit the resort city of Sharm el-Sheikh, Egypt, killing over 80 people. On 14 Aug, a flight crashed in Greece killing 121 passengers and crew. On 16 Aug 2005, another flight crashed in Venezuela, killing 160 passengers and crew. On 29 Aug 2005, Hurricane Katrina made landfall along the U.S. Gulf Coast, causing severe damage, killing over a thousand people and dealing an estimated

Billions Dollar damage. On 31 Aug 2005, a stampede at the Al-Aaimmah bridge in Baghdad, Iraq, killed 953. On 08 Oct 2005, a 7.6 Mw Kashmir earthquake struck Pak Occupied Kashmir, killing more than 86,000 people and displacing several million more.

This time the planet position will be worse when Rahu and Saturn conjunct in Pisces sign and Kaal Sarp Yoga is formed. At the mundane level, there may be several calamities, accidents and disasters. However, life continues as nature causes destruction to keep a balance in eco system.

15 May to 16 Jul 2025

Jupiter Sun conjunction in Gemini, 15 June to 16 July 2025 will bring positive results for financial sectors. This will be time for the Banking sector to grow and accordingly, stock prices of Banks may notice a spike. This is a time of positivity for the Public. There will be an increase in financial status. Industries will grow with the support of the government. Remember that before this period, there will be a major correction in the market.

07 June to 28 July 2025

Mars Ketu conjunction from 07 June to 28 July 2025 is being formed in Leo sign, fiery sign. Ketu and Mars energies may result in fire, terrorist attacks, and natural disasters in mountainous terrain in a few countries. Leo is a fire sign and Mars is a fiery planet with Ketu, a planet of destruction that will affect nature, forests and land. There may be landslides, and settlement of ground resulting in damage to buildings. Sun and Mars both represent energy. This period also coincides with the summer season when you find fire incidents in several places. This period may also witness air accidents, train accidents, industrial accidents, or major fire incidents.

17 Aug to 15 Sep 2025

Sun and Ketu conjunction is being formed in the Leo sign from 17 Aug to 16 Sep 2025 may bring turbulence for ruling governments. In some states, there may be trading of elected candidates to form various alliances, destabilise the ruling party and form their government. All over the world, you may notice that opposition parties may try to destabilise the ruling government by ethical or unethical means. Terrorist activities will emerge in a new form and higher intensity. Sun is eclipsed by Ketu and indicates trouble in law and order, the death of a popular world leader and an increase in terrorist activities. To control the law-and-order situation, governments have to take some strong steps which can cause mass unrest.

Leo is related to the stomach and digestive system. Diseases related to the stomach may surface as epidemics during this period.

16 Nov 2025 to 14 Jan 2026

Sun-Mars conjunction is being formed in Scorpio and later Sagittarius sign. Sun and Mars energies indicate that the authorities become tyrants and make decisions that may not be democratic or for the welfare of the public. They force their ways to achieve their targets. This period may witness some major clashes between govt and various rebel groups. This may turn out to be violent in Nov 2025. It can have some connection with new laws which will be passed by governments in various countries. Those laws may be against religious conversion or migration-related. Like Europe or Western countries such as the US, the UK may impose certain restrictions on the migration of refugees, population control etc which may give rise to anti-government campaigns. In India, these could be related to the construction of the temple at the site which has been converted to a mosque after the demolition of the temple. Kashi Vishwanath or Mathura temple may come into focus during this period. Govt may take action on certain parties based on their involvement in corruption or anti-national activities.

I have endeavored to provide predictions for each zodiac sign, which should be considered with both your Moon Sign and Lagna. You can explore how this upcoming transit might introduce new opportunities or challenges in your life and the lives of your family members.

Aries Sign as Whole

Aries is the first constellation of the zodiac, located in the Northern celestial hemisphere between Pisces to the west and Taurus to the east. It lies between 0 degrees to 30 degrees of the Zodiac. Aries has three prominent stars forming an asterism, designated Alpha (Hamal) Beta (Sheratan) and Gama. In the constellation, Aries covers three Nakshatras, Ashwini, Bharani and one pada of Krittika. As per the Sun astrology, people born during the period 21 Mar to 19 April fall under the Aries sign. In Vedic astrology, the Aries sign starts from 13 to 14 April every year.

Alphabets associated with Aries Sign are Chu, Choo, Che, Chay, Cho, La, Lha, Li, Lee, Lhi, Lu, Loo, Lhu, Le, Lay, Lo.

Aries is a fiery, moveable, male, odd, rajjoguna, Kshatriya class zodiac sign having Pitta nature and is linked to the east direction. Aries represent youth and fiery attributes, it has a tall stature and is associated with the red color.

Aries is governed by the planet Mars. Mars is the Commander of the Army in the celestial kingdom and is associated with action, offensive capabilities, initiative, energy, pro-activeness, and anger.

Each zodiac sign is associated with a character or symbol that describes them. The zodiac symbol of the Aries star sign is the curving horns of a sheep, the Ram. The Aries symbol signifies stubbornness, relentless effort, rage, and driving energy. This symbol is the reason for Arians are persistent, stubborn and making continuous efforts to explore new heights in life.

Aries sign is governed by the Fire element, which signifies full of action, initiative, quick-tempered, impulsive, passionate, assertive, and competitive nature. The fire signs actively seek and enjoy being in the spotlight. The Arians shine with an intense inner drive that pushes them to pursue their goals swiftly and decisively.

Aries, as the pioneers of the zodiac, with fire element have the fire qualities with the key phrase "I AM!" Their ruling planet, Mars, instills virtues of action and courage but may lead to defects like arrogance. Being the first Sign of the Zodiac, people born under this Sign see themselves as the "First" and are born leaders, first in line to get things going. You will find that for any assignment, the Arians will volunteer themselves and are always ready to take risks, initiative and lead others. Whether or not everything gets done is another question altogether.

Arians can fearlessly step into the unknown as symbolized by the ram. They thrive on action and enjoy exploring new territories. They are full of energy and love embracing new possibilities. Arians act quickly, sometimes without fully thinking things through, but their enthusiasm and initiative often lead to exciting discoveries. Their approach to life is all about living and playing with intensity.

Arians display typical traits of dynamism, impulsiveness, quarrelsomeness, selfishness, aggression, enthusiasm, and forcefulness. Their interests revolve around themselves and their motto in life is "I" only. They like to handle difficult assignments which may pose certain challenges. They possess strong willpower and self-confidence which diverts them to handle warlike situations.

They are born leader and like to lead others due to their confidence, initiative and ability to take risks. Being the first sign in the Zodiac, Aries adopts a "lead-the-way-and-get-things-started" attitude, influenced by Mars, the ruling planet. Arians exhibit impressive leadership qualities and personal magnetism, often rallying others against seemingly insurmountable odds. They prefer taking charge and may struggle with following directions. As natural leaders, Aries are responsible and genuinely care for those whom they lead. Despite their impulsive nature, Aries possesses excellent organizational skills and dislikes clutter. They should be given an independent task.

Arians has a proactive and competitive nature, often striving for first place always without considering the rights and feelings of others. They rarely admit defeat, persisting in their efforts until success or demise. The key to their success lies in balancing their assertiveness with diplomacy and tact. Aries individuals can achieve remarkable success, if they learn to respect and love others while acting with wisdom.

Arians are known for their confidence, optimism, courage, passion, and determination. They thrive in leadership roles and are drawn to individual sports and physical challenges. Aries is associated with new beginnings, symbolized by the ram, reflecting ambition, impulsiveness, adventure, and energy.

Aries individuals are often intelligent and innovative, generating new ideas that they are eager to put into action. They are inclined to initiate projects and look for immediate results. Their impatience, however, can lead to agitation if immediate results are not achieved. They may lose interest and start looking to initiate a new project with new challenges. They are likely to fail in routine or mundane activities, as these do not pose any challenges.

One drawback is their tendency to focus solely on the goal during projects, potentially appearing selfish to others. Impatience is a common trait, and if their hard work isn't promptly recognized, Arians can become sarcastic and rude.

Though their impulsive nature can lead to quick decisions, they embody a "live hard, play hard" philosophy. They are proactive individuals, eager to contribute and make things happen.

Arains like to be involved in activities that are filled with adventure, risk, action, physical effort, and energy. That may relate to their work area or their sports or hobbies. their tendency to focus solely on the goal may lead to perceived selfishness. Arians are driven by strong initiative, courage, and determination, contributing significantly to their projects. The fiery element of Aries symbolizes assertive "I" energy, instilling tension, passion, and a need for independence.

While Arians can be strong, enthusiastic, and forward-looking, they may exhibit tactlessness, impatience, and a myopic view. Their eagerness to achieve goals can lead to nervousness or irritability if things don't progress quickly. Uncultivated Arians may struggle with doubt and fear, and efforts to express themselves authentically are essential for personal growth.

To summarise an Arian on the positive side, he is quite strong, enthusiastic, forward-looking, and not easily discouraged by temporary setbacks. He has a strong personality, is clear about his goals and even is a source of inspiration for others. He likes to live a life filled with risk, adventure, action and luxuries. His quick and active mind keeps him busy. He is imaginative and inventive. He likes to explore the world by traveling, enhancing his knowledge and communicating. He always seems to remain young and optimistic.

To summarise an Arian on the negative side, is egoistic, rude, arrogant, and not tactful in communication. He is quick and impatient and so occasionally fails in planning and completing the task. If the task is not filled with challenges, he may leave it incomplete. His motto is "I" so he may ignore the feelings of others. He does not like to take orders and may be a subordinate tough to handle. At times Arien is too impulsive. He can occasionally be stubborn and refuse to listen to reason.

Aries Predictions: 2025

Aries is the first zodiac sign, associated with the fire element. People born under this sign are usually determined and assertive due to their ruling planet Mars. At the beginning of the year, you will experience a boost in courage and valour as Mars, the ruling planet of your zodiac sign, will aspect the tenth house, the house of Karmas. As the period progresses, with the transit of Jupiter in May, you can expect to encounter new opportunities and challenges in the field of communications and professional life.

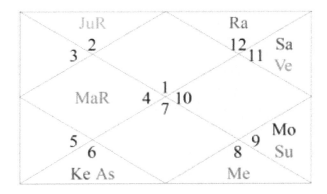

As per planetary position till 29 Mar 2025, the period will bring favorable results in finances and family affairs. This can be time for auspicious outcomes such as increased wealth, career success, and happiness in personal life.

On 14 May 2025, Jupiter will transit to Gemini which may not be much beneficial for the Aries natives. On 18 Oct 2025, Jupiter transit to Cancer.

On 29 Mar 2025, Saturn will transit to the twelfth house and Sade Sati of Aries will commence. Rahu being in the eleventh house after 18 May 2025 will motivate the person to take initiative but the outcome may not be as desired. There may be problems on the financial and health front.

In the second part of the year, Rahu in Aquarius in the eleventh house and Ketu in Leo in the fifth house will help to mitigate the negative effects of Shani Sade Sati. With the influence of Jupiter on the ninth house, Aries people will find themselves drawn towards a more spiritual path, leading to positive outcomes.

Once Saturn goes retrograde from 13 July to 28 Nov 2025 and Jupiter retrograde from 11 Nov 2025 to 11 Mar 2026, you will find that problems may further increase and that is the period to be a little cautious. I think remedies of Saturn may be helpful to ease some issues.

The period after 18 May 2025, is going to bring good news when it comes to your relationship and career. Your relationship with friends and associates will improve invariably. There might be some challenges that you have to encounter after the middle of the year in your career, however, there is nothing to be worried about. These hurdles will remain for a temporary period. You must keep control of your negative thoughts. To accomplish your achievements, you must work harder. You are advised to have control over your temper, or you might end up losing some favorable connections with your friends and family.

After May 2025, the period will be conducive to spiritual activities, and you may consider planning visits to religious places. However, be mindful of increased travel expenses during this time.

In your personal life, your bond with your partner will be strong, and both of you will demonstrate loyalty and faithfulness towards each other. This year will bring you closer together, fostering a deeper connection. Any feelings of loneliness you may have experienced in the past will dissipate, and you might find a desirable love partner entering your life. There are going to be some challenges in your relationship and career. If you lose control of emotions and temper will end up losing everything have been trying to build. Be patient and try to be optimistic.

Profession

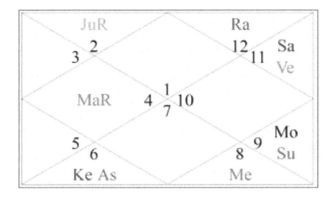

Your career and business are off to a positive start, thanks to Jupiter's transit in the second house of your chart since April 2024.

Till 29 Mar 2025, Saturn, the Karam Phal Data, will be positioned in the eleventh house of your astrological chart. The eleventh house is associated with gains, and when Saturn is in its sign, it becomes beneficial and will give you success in your professional life. You'll have the opportunity to meet influential people who will impact your career significantly. These influential people may be from different caste colour or community. You may encounter helpful individuals, possibly of the opposite sex, in your workplace who will aid in your professional growth. Learning from these authorities will enhance your efficiency and showcase your talents.

The period holds promising prospects for launching your brand in a different company. Any brand related to unorthodox practices or items may provide your career a new boost. Rahu in the twelfth house, indicates that you can have growth by unconventional approach. Rahu is the technology and you have to adopt new technology, make connections with foreign traders, and look for opportunities in the import and export business. There are potential opportunities for financial gain in the business you have been working on, indicating a favorable time to make progress in your professional endeavors. For those who are doing business in import and export, Rahu connects you to foreign lands and gives a boost to business. You will have the ability to overcome your enemies, although they may continue to pose challenges. Aries individuals are naturally determined and fierce fighters due to their Martian attributes, giving them an inherent spirit to confront and triumph over obstacles.

Those who are dealing with business related to import export, technology, hospitals or the hotel industry may gain during this period. Ketu being in the sixth house, you will be able to be victorious in competitions and competitive bids. Remember Ketu is in the Virgo sign, and whenever there is any competitive bidding or competition, you should worship Maa Kaali. Taking wishes from a woman will increase the chances of success. Once Ketu moves to Leo sign on 18 May 2025, the advantage of having a killer spirit in competition will fade away.

The period between 29 Mar to 18 May 2025, when Rahu and Saturn conjunct in the twelfth house, the situation is going to be worse. With Saturn transit to the twelfth house on 29 Mar 2025, your Sade Sati first phase will start. Saturn placement and with Rahu conjunction is not auspicious here and will cause confusion, indecisiveness, worries and anxieties. There may be poverty, loss in business and a sharp decline in income, heavy and uncontrolled expenditure and aimless travels involving trouble. You may be transferred to another location and may have conflict with relatives. There may be unpleasant changes in life and losses due to litigations.

The native may have to incur losses, heavy expenses, face an allegation or inquiry or disappointment in his efforts. Be careful during the period 12 Feb to 14 Apr 2025, 17 Aug to 17 Sep 2025.

For Aries natives with the lord of the tenth house in the twelfth house after 29 Mar 2025, success will require letting go of any laziness and putting in extra effort. Also, the Sade Sati of Shani will start. During the Saturn retrograde or Jupiter retrograde period, results may be a little unpredictable.

On 14 May 2025, Jupiter moves to the third house in Gemini till 18 Oct 2025 and thereafter to Cancer, your new business idea is set to progress, and launching your venture will prove fruitful, leading to significant profits. Embrace this success to seek even better opportunities. Nevertheless, there will be challenging days, but don't lose heart; keep moving forward.

After 18 May 2025, their social status may find an uplift. Those who are in the public domain, in politics, in social groups, or running some social media ads on YouTube, Instagram etc may find a boost in their followers. Those who are in Politics may find success and better recognition in their field.

Saturn goes for retrogradation from 13 July to 28 Nov 2025 for a period of 139 days. Be prepared for that and keep your reserves to cater to a rainy day. Sade Sati of Saturn with retrograde Saturn may bring lot of challenges and obstacles in all spheres.

Finances

Jupiter will be in the second house till 14 May 2025, and then it will transit in the third house for one year. It indicates that the period till 14 May will be quite positive for financial aspects. You may have a lot of savings and finances in general will be comfortable despite heavy expenditures. With the Rahu in the twelfth house, your expenditure will also increase. The expenditure could be on your enjoyment, charity, travel abroad or travel to religious places, medical expenses or clearing a debt. House renovation or expansion is also the reason for higher expenditure. Some legal issues related to the professional front may be one of the reasons for higher expenses. You may be required to spend some money on your siblings. You may do some rash buying without any deliberation. It can cause financial problems so plan the budget accordingly. However, there is no need to worry till 29 Mar 2025, as Jupiter will be free from any affliction in the Taurus Sign and indicate that you will have sufficient savings.

The financial situation will be stressful after 29 Mar 2025. There may be certain financial losses that will affect your savings. Expenditures may surpass income and savings.

Till 18 May 2025, the Rahu aspect is the eighth house and Jupiter in the Taurus aspect the eighth house. You may gain from secret financial dealings, inheritance, undesirable channels, stock markets, gambling or mutual funds. He will earn from the financial management of other people. This period will be good for long-term investing in the share market as well however retro movement of planets should be considered before making any decision. You may get some ancestral property or gains from stocks, insurance or long-term mutual funds.

After 14 May 2025, Jupiter will shift to the third house and as Sade Sati begins on 29 Mar 2025, you might encounter some financial challenges, so it's important to be cautious about your finances. Before making any risky decisions, carefully consider the potential outcomes, as there's a chance of losing money. While your income will be satisfactory, your expenses could also rise. To manage this, you'll need to control your spending to align with your earnings. Your steady income will allow you to save while considering investments that hold substantial value. Despite increased spending, focus on channeling your financial resources into meaningful and enduring assets, rather than short-term indulgences. Shani Sade Sati will churn out the entire finances in the next 2.5 years, so plan accordingly.

During the period 09 Oct 2024 to 04 Feb 2025, 11 Nov 2025 to 11 Mar 2026, be careful while making any financial decisions However it is advised to not do any panic buying. Do not give a loan and avoid taking a loan as it will take time to clear the loan. You may buy an item on EMI during this period as a remedy. Any wrong decision taken during the period 09 Oct 2024 to 04 Feb 2025 may cause financial distress later so be careful.

Health

The year is set to begin on a positive note, with Jupiter in the second house providing you protection from any chronic disease but minor health issues cannot be ruled out. Jupiter will aspect the eighth house, potentially leading to medical expenditures. Digestive and stomach-related issues might arise, and recovery could take time.

With Jupiter in the second house till 14 May 2025, be mindful of your diet as it may increase, leading to weight-related health issues. Fasting on Thursdays or a day of your choice can be beneficial for health-related matters. Making changes in your eating habits, along with regular exercise and weekly fasting, can improve your overall well-being. Health should be a top priority, so ensure you follow through with medical check-ups as advised and stay proactive about your health.

The situation will be worse when Saturn joins the Rahu from 29 Mar to 18 May 2025. Energies of two malefic planets, Rahu and Saturn working in the twelfth house will cause stress and agony which can cause deprivation of sleep. On 14 May 2025, Jupiter transits to Gemini, the third house. Health issues may get activated and need your attention. This period may be crucial as any problem arising during this period will not be diagnosed easily. Aries may have problems related to knees and legs. The twelfth house also relates to the left eye and Saturn here may cause eye infection or some issues. If you are undergoing a Period or sub-period of Saturn, you may require medical attention. It will be difficult to diagnose the disease. You should be careful about your health. Do not ignore any health-related warnings as visits to hospitals and expenditures are likely during that period.

After 18 May 2025, if the natal chart is strong then nothing to worry otherwise be mindful of issues related to the digestive system, constipation, injury to legs and infection to eyes, especially for individuals with afflicted Saturn in their birth chart. They should be particularly cautious about their legs during that period. If any health issues arise, they will take a longer time to recover.

Those having any health issues need to be careful during the period 13 July to 28 Nov 2025, this will be the sensitive period when some health issues may trouble you if you are having any earlier health issues.

Love Life and Marriage

With the onset of the year 2025, Jupiter is in transit in the second house till 14 May 2025, which is considered the "marka" house, implying it may not be as beneficial for married life, especially for females. Jupiter's positioning in the eighth position from the seventh house, the natural significator of marriage for females, could lead to challenges in married life for some individuals. As Jupiter will be in the second house from 01 May 2024 to 14 May 2025, the period is not positive from the marriage perspective. Interestingly, if the marriage happens to a life partner having a different nationality, caste, culture or society the marriage will be successful otherwise there will be problems. For those who want to go to a foreign country after marrying NRI, this is the right opportunity.

The twelfth house also signifies pleasure from sex, so Rahu's placement here indicates unconventional or greater expectations from a partner for sex which may not be satisfied. The native may look for sex partners outside the social norms. He may be carrying out expenditures for the same. The period will be quite prominent from 29 Mar to 18 May 2025, when Saturn and Rahu conjunct in the twelfth house.

For married people, period till 14 May 2025, you may find some suffocation in your love relations. That may be due to the reason that you have started having big plans and you find your love relations are not matching your expectations, so you trying to avoid meeting them. Take your time and don't rush into matters of love. Building a stable relationship requires careful analysis of the person you are interested in. Saturn's aspect on the fifth house puts caution and delays in the love affairs. Romance should unfold naturally; avoid trying to force it, as it may only create distance between you and your partner. Instead, focus on communication and understanding each other's personal space.

Period 27 Feb to 18 May 2025 is a period of caution for those who have weak Venus in their natal chart. During this period there can be some health or sexual issues for those who have weak Venus in their birth chart.

For unmarried, the period until 18 May 2024 is not very conducive for marriage. However, after 18 May 2025, Rahu and Jupiter aspect on the seventh house will open the opportunity for marriage for unmarried people. However natal chart and major and minor Dasha should support that. The next year is quite positive for unmarried Aries and those who want to get married. They will get an opportunity for sure and they need to encash that. I will advise to unmarried that now not to delay their marriage proposals during the period Jupiter is in the third house. Jupiter will be in the fourth house for a short period of 18 Oct to 5 Dec 2025 which again may show some reluctance in forming yogas for marriage.

The period from 07 June to 28 July 2025, when Ketu conjuncts with Venus in the Leo sign, is a difficult time as it indicates problems in a love relationship. Extra care and attention are needed during this period to counter any challenges that may arise. Do not overreact in a love relationship during this period.

Progeny

For Aries native, the period till 18 May 2025 is good in matters of progeny. The period is positive to conceive and deliver but after 18 May 2025, the period may not be positive as the fifth house will be occupied by Ketu and may delay or destroy the progeny. The problems are more for male children. They may require the medical support or remedies of Ketu in the conception and retention of the foetus.

In the period from 7 June to 28 July 2025, Mars will be in the fifth house and conjunct with Ketu. It further complicates the problem in first pregnancy. Aries needs to be cautious in this regard. It is better to get their natal horoscope checked as the natal chart is more helpful in making predictions.

Education

For Aries native, the period till 18 May 2025 is good in matters of education. They will get the results after hard work because Saturn also watches them from the eleventh house. Those who are looking to go abroad for higher education may find a positive period. Rahu transit in the twelfth house provides an opportunity for students to go abroad for higher education.

After 18 May 2025, they find certain distractions or would like to change the subjects. Those who have a strong background may do well and shift to a foreign country or place away from their home for further education. Saturn will create obstacles in their Visa applications. Remember you have to work hard in education as success will not be easy.

Spiritualism

In the initial part of 2025, Jupiter in the second house and Rahu in the 12th house, you may have a strong desire for spiritual growth and a quest for higher understanding. You may be attracted to spiritual practices and may have deep insights into spiritual matters. You may develop certain psychic abilities or have an interest in the occult.

After 29 Mar 2025, Rahu will be afflicted by Saturn and then it can cause problems in these areas. You may be led to delusions or a distorted understanding of spirituality. You need to keep a balance and not get carried away by your spiritual pursuits, as this can lead to problems in other areas of your life. You may be drawn to unhealthy or unwise spiritual practices or beliefs, or to become too focused on material gains and pleasure at the expense of your spiritual development. You may have to struggle with issues related to your subconscious mind and your past actions. They may also face challenges in their spiritual pursuits and may be prone to illusion and delusion. You may lose your interest in spirituality as expenses and health may be issues of concern. You may be more focused on making money and stop doing charity or donation.

After 18 May 2025, Rahu moves to the eleventh house, the native will be busy in his social circles and friends and may lose interest in his advancement in spiritual activities. Ketu in the fifth house forces him to the spiritual path but only those who are firm in their commitment will stay on the path and the weaker will divert. As Sade Sati on Aries will start, the person may get into different problems that disturb his peace of mind and he may feel detached from God. He may feel that God is unjust or does not exist. This is the beauty of the Sade Sati period. Subsequently, they are so engrossed in religious remedies and stop doing their Karmas considering that nothing is working out.

Aries Monthwise Predictions

After going through predictions in general, let us find out certain periods where some changes will be expected. I wanted to be more specific but as there is no fixed pattern to consider the timelines, the best way was to take transit of the Sun, which takes 30 days and then include the transit of other planets, during that period. Considering the effect of conjunctions of planets during that period further helps to reach better accuracy. Major Planets such as Saturn, Rahu, Ketu and Jupiter are going to transit for longer durations and affect the life path. But within that longer period, good or bad events will occur based on the transit of inner planets. I could only think of this as the best option. Your comments or feedback on this is always welcome to improve the procedures. This is in consideration of the transit of the Sun and other planets in general.

You should consider that these predictions are based on general planetary movement and do not consider the natal chart of individuals. Period, sub-period and planet position in the natal chart have major significance and vary from person to person and even twins have a lot of variations. It is better to consult an astrologer for a personalised annual horoscope. It does not cost much but gives you some psychological support and some warning for which you can take some precautions. Also, remember that there is no remedy for fixed or incurable Karmas as you have to face them in this life cycle or the next one.

Period: 01 Jan to 13 Jan 2025

The planetary position on 01 Jan 2025, as Sun is in transit in Sagittarius, the planetary position for the Aries sign will be as per the chart: -

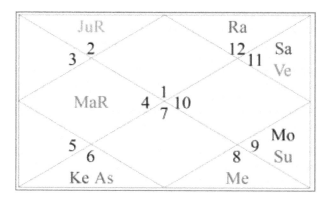

During this period, retrograde Mercury will turn to direct on 16 Dec 2024 and transit to Sagittarius on 4 Jan 2025, Jupiter as has been retrograde since 09 Oct 2024 in Taurus sign will continue to be retrograde till 04 Feb 2025. Mars has been in retrograde motion in Cancer since 7 Dec 2024 and will continue in retrograde motion.

Venus will be in conjunction with Saturn in the Aquarius sign from 28 Dec 2024 to 28 Jan 2025.

During this period, the Sun will be in transit in the ninth house, the house of religion, morality, higher education and father. Your focus area will be your parents, long travels, religious activities, legal issues and even health issues of self or parents. You may be required to travel a lot for business or adventure activities. You might feel the urge to get out and explore your immediate environment. If you're involved in the touring job, you may be required to visit long distances or even foreign places. I find these tours or visits may not be conducive as fruitful as per your expectations. You may be carrying out a lot of expenditures which will impinge your savings. Even credit card bills or expenditures carried out during parties of New Year or travels in Dec 2024 need to be settled in this month.

You will get happiness from brothers and sisters and even your children, however expectations from them may lead to stress. Avoid arrogance with the seniors and your father as your stubbornness and aggressive attitude can land you antagonising the elders and superiors.

Your connection to a foreign land using visiting there for tourism or higher education is quite possible during this time. You may connect with people from different backgrounds or engage in activities that broaden your cultural awareness.

You may find some opportunities which you have missed earlier. Some land deals which have been pending may come up for discussion again. You may need to travel for the purchase of property. There may be some legal issues related to property. You need to be careful while signing any legal documents or contracts. Mercury is in the eighth house till 04 Jan 2025, aspected by Retro Jupiter and Rahu creating a situation where you will tend to make wrong decisions regarding investment. Do not get lured by the property dealers' claims or investment advisors. Any decision regarding property needs to be re-analyzed. Avoid any investment at least till 04 Feb 2025.

During the period you have to address issues of relationships, partnerships, marriage, and one-on-one connections. There could be some challenges or conflicts that need to be addressed and resolved during this period. If you are married, there may be some problems in your married life. It's advised to be cautious and avoid unnecessary arguments or conflicts with your life partner during this time to prevent any trouble. Take care of the health of your family members during this period. You may go through some emotional turmoil on the family front. Those having high Blood pressure, Cholesterol and heart issues, need to remain cool and attentive to their health issues.

Period: 14 Jan to 12 Feb 2025

The planetary position for Aries Sign as of 14 Jan 2025 will be as under: -

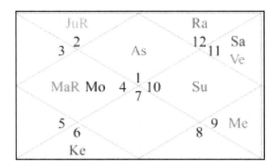

During this period, Mars in retrograde movement transits to Gemini on 21 Jan 2025, Mercury transit to Capricorn on 24 Jan 2025, Venus transits to Pisces on 28 Jan 2025 sign till 31 May 2025 and then Mercury shifts in Aquarius on 11 Feb 2025.

Conjunction of planets Venus and Saturn in Aquarius from 28 Dec to 28 Jan 2025, Sun and Mercury in Capricorn from 24 Jan to 11 Feb 2025. Venus and Rahu in Pisces from 28 Jan to 31 May 2025.

Sun transit in the tenth house, house of profession is poised to bring positive transformations in one's professional life. It can lead to the individual earning name, fame, reputation and acknowledgment due to their dedicated work ethic and professional conduct. Those contemplating a career change might find a fitting job opportunity. During this period, you will remain connected to your professional activities. You may get a leadership role at work, or you may even start or activate any of your ventures. You will be successful in all ventures that you are planning and making a sincere effort. Remember tenth house is the house of Karmas and you have to work hard. Success will not come automatically but if you make an effort, you will be victorious. You will benefit from your higher authorities, friends and relations. You may regain your lost position during this period. You will be able to showcase your leadership qualities during this period.

The health of the mother or brother can be an issue of concern. Expenditures will be on the higher side.

After 21 Jan 2025, there may be a dispute regarding inheritance, insurance or some commission due to him. You may find some issues of dispute with your siblings or father. You will be required to travel for your professional reasons.

The period 28 Jan to 31 May 2025, due to Venus Rahu conjunction in the twelfth house, you need to be cautious about your relationship. The health of a life partner can be an issue of concern. Your expenditure is likely to be on luxuries, travel and enjoyment. Those who are unmarried may find matches from different castes, colors or countries. Those who are working in a foreign country may find a life partner from a different culture.

Period: 13 Feb to 14 Mar 2025

For Aries Ascendant, the Planetary position as of 13 Feb 2025 when the Sun transits to Aquarius will be as under:-

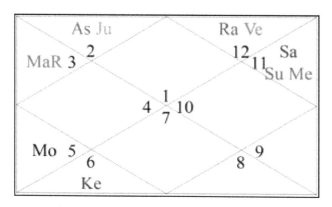

During this period, Mercury transits to Pisces on 27 Feb 2025. Venus will become retrograde in Pisces from 2 Mar 2025 to 13 Apr 2025. Mars will become direct on 24 Feb 2025 in Gemini.

In Pisces sign, Rahu is conjunct with Venus in Pisces from 28 Jan to 27 Feb 2025. In Aquarius, Saturn and Mercury conjunct from 11 Feb to 12 Feb 2025, Saturn, Mercury and Sun from 12 Feb to 27 Feb 2025 and then Saturn and Sun from 27 Feb to 14 Mar 2025.

During this period, the Sun will be in transit in the eleventh house over Saturn. The eleventh house is the house of gains and social networking. You will be ambitious and aggressive in your professional life but still tend to have a vast and diverse social network. You will be friendly, outgoing, and enjoy being part of various groups and communities. You will have ambitious goals and dreams which you want to achieve. You may not get the requisite support from the higher authorities, government officials and even your father. There may be a clash of ego with the higher-ups. However, to achieve success you have to work hard and also remain grounded and humble. Relations with your father or the health of father may be an issue of concern for you. Those having a period or sub period of Sun or Saturn may face some form of humiliation or allegation.

Do not take any risk of changing the job during his period. Any promotion or appreciation you were expecting may not happen as per your expectations.

There are chances of the person taking risks in activities that can be adventurous games, gambling or the stock market. Avoid assertive behaviour in guidance and discipline their children, emphasizing qualities like self-confidence and independence. You may not be satisfied with the achievements of your children. I suppose exam pressure may be the reason or the results of their academic performance may not be as per your expectations causing stressful relations.

The period 28 Jan to 31 May 2025, due to Venus Rahu conjunction in the twelfth house and Mercury conjunct on 27 Feb 2025 further Venus going retrograde from 2 Mar to 13 Apr 2025, a person may have issues in married life or regarding the health of life partner. There can be some communication problems with a life partner or in a love relationship. Those who are in a love relationship may be cheated or may cheat. There will be a loss of trust in the relationship. The health of the life partner can be an issue of concern. You may be required to spend your savings in the hospital.

Period: 15 Mar to 13 Apr 2025

The Planetary position for Aries Sign as of 15 Mar 2025 will be as under:-

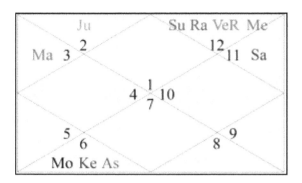

During this period, a major transit of Saturn is happening when Saturn transits to Pisces on 29 Mar 2025 for 2 years and 2 months till 3 June 2027. This is a major transit when Sade Sati of Aries will commence and Capricorn will be free from Shani Sade Sati. Mercury will be in retro in Pisces from 15 Mar to 07 Apr 2025. Mars will enter Cancer on 3 Apr 2025 till 7 June 2025. Venus will be direct in Pisces on 13 Apr 2025. Rahu transit to Aquarius and Ketu to Leo on 18 May 2025.

Conjunction In Pisces, Rahu Venus, Mercury and Sun conjunct from 14 Mar to 29 Mar 2025. After Saturn's transit to Pisces on 29 Mar 2025, five planets Rahu, Saturn, Mercury, Venus and Sun will be in conjunction from 29 Mar to 14 Apr 2025. Kaal Sarp Yoga is being formed on 29 Mar 2025.

Rahu Sun conjunction is being formed in the Pisces sign in the twelfth house. Rahu occults the Sun and creates a false ego. This false ego may result in making wrong decisions which may be quite problematic at a later stage. This period also indicates a lack of life force means energy due to health issues of self or family members, especially your father. You may be required to visit the hospital to look after some of your near and dear and carry out expenditures. Your relationship with your siblings, colleagues or your life partner may be troublesome during this period. You need to be cautious while signing any legal documents or any loan offer.

Those who are in the public domain and not having transparent dealings may be implicated with charges of corruption or malpractice. Certain issues may emerge related to health and even on the professional front.

Due to various challenges at the professional or home front, you may start exploring the deeper meaning in life and explore the realms of the subconscious and spirituality. You may tend to introspection and privacy and would like to spend time alone.

Those who want to settle abroad may find an opportunity. Students may find it an opportunity for higher studies abroad. Those dealing with foreign companies in the profession may find the period quite positive. You may also get an opportunity to travel abroad for official work or leisure. Your employer may like to send you to negotiate a deal with any client. You may be traveling to a spiritual place or exploring a spiritual journey during this period.

Mercury dictates your decision taking capabilities and during this period decisions taken may not be conducive and correct. The period may affect the results as perceived and bring challenges in your education, love relationship, speculations, finances, inheritance. Avoid any major decisions related to family activities, marriage and investment during this retro period. There may be some legal issues related to inheritance. You need to be careful while signing any legal documents or contracts. Do not get lured by the property dealers' claims or investment advisors. Legal matters or negotiations with others may come into the picture more prominently, but the outcomes may not always align with your desires. You may be faced with opportunities or challenges regarding financial matters, such as loans or debts.

On 29 Mar 2025, Saturn joins the Rahu Sun, Mercury, and Venus's conjunction. A Kaal Sarp yoga is being formed. Apart from this, Sade Sati of Aries sign will commence and a period of 7.5 years of churning your deeds start. If the Karmas (deeds) are good, you may gain immensely and if Karmas are corrupt or bad, be ready for the justice of Saturn who is a little tough to handle.

I find the period of Kaal Sarp, 29 Mar to 13 Sep 2025, will be quite a sensitive period which may find several untoward incidences worldwide. All the planets except the Moon will be in the grip of Rahu and Ketu. You need to be cautious and avoid any major decisions during this period. The period till 18 May 2025 may not be overall good for everyone as there will be a lot of turbulence, and loss of lives in society due to accidents and natural calamities. Major Sunami may cause damage alongside coastal areas.

Period: 14 Apr to 14 May 2025

The Planetary position for Aries Sign as of 14 Mar 2025 will be as under: -

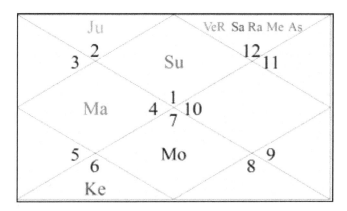

During this period, Mercury transit to Aries on 7 May 2025, Jupiter transits to Gemini on 14 May 2025.

In Pisces, Rahu, Saturn, Mercury and Venus conjunct from 14 Apr 2025 to 07 May 2025. Rahu, Saturn and Venus from 7 May to 18 May 2025. In Aries, Sun and Mercury from 7 May to 15 May 2025

During this period, Sun transit in Lagna and you can expect a lot of positivity and numerous opportunities coming your way. Your confidence will soar, and you'll feel more optimistic about life. This positive outlook will make you eager to take on challenges and go after your goals. Those in politics may find the period quite positive for them. New opportunities will open, leading to growth in various aspects of your life. Your efforts may be recognized, and you could see success in your endeavours. People around you will look up to you for guidance and inspiration, and you might find yourself leading important projects.

During this period, your primary emphasis will be on self-health, self-growth, matters related to relationships, partnerships, marriage, and one-to-one connections. You're expected to consider your significant relationships, including those with your spouse, romantic partner, or close business associates. You might feel more assertive in your relationships and express your individuality within the context of your partnerships This attitude of yours could create some challenges or conflicts with your life partner or business partner.

You will be ambitious and will have the courage to express yourself and lead others. You would like to explore and broaden your horizons. You might feel drawn to travel or seek out learning experiences to expand your knowledge. You'll feel a strong urge to improve yourself and gain more knowledge about life. You could achieve significant milestones and make progress toward your long-term goals. This newfound self-assurance will contribute to your overall well-being and success.

Your optimistic attitude will have a beneficial impact on those around you, inspiring them to be more confident in their pursuits. Opportunities and resources may increase, bringing good fortune your way.

Due to your busy schedule or ego issues, your interests towards sexual interest will be lacking which further may affect your relationship with your life partner. Sun is a separatist planet and its aspect over the seventh house creates a lot of ego and anger issues resulting in disagreement with the life partner.

Mars is currently in debilitation and aspected by the Rahu in the fourth house. It is advisable to steer clear of property-related dealings during this period. It is important to pay attention to your mother's health and well-being. Avoid anger and ego issues at home as they may be the cause of disputes at home. Parental property disputes may come up during this transit. Better to wait rather than look for a resolution during this period.

As you are aware, due to the Venus Rahu conjunction in the twelfth house till 31 May 2025, a few of Aries may be attracted to some old friend of the opposite sex which may result in a disturbance of peace of mind, and family relations and even cause heavy expenditure. Those who have a strong mental character may not be affected. Take care of the health of your life partner and control the expenditures.

Period: 15 May to 14 June 2025

Planetary position on 14 May 2024, at the time Sun transit to Taurus will be as per the chart:-

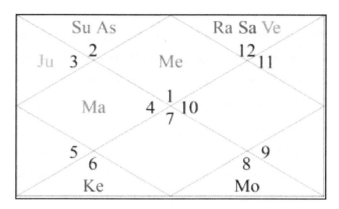

During the upcoming period, Jupiter transit to Gemini on 14 May 2025, Rahu transit to Aquarius and Ketu in Leo on 18 May 2025, Mercury in Taurus on 23 May 2025, and Venus will enter Aries on 06 June 2025. Mercury transit to Gemini on 6 June 2025, and Mars enters Leo on 7 June 2025.

In Pisces, Rahu, Saturn and Venus from 7 May to 18 May 205, Venus and Saturn from 18 May to 31 May 2025. In Taurus, the Sun and Mercury conjunct from 23 May to 6 June 2025. In Gemini, Jupiter and Mercury conjunct from 6 June to 15 June 2025. In Leo sign, Ketu and Mars conjunct from 7 June to 28 July 2025.

Sun transit in the second house, house of speech, family and finances will create a lot of opportunities or challenges regarding financial matters, such as inheritance, loans, debts, or joint ventures. Investments in stocks or mutual funds may be in a turbulence mode and you need to be watchful. Your communication skills will be appreciated by others and you will prove yourself as an eloquent speaker. You will get an opportunity to interact with your family members. Any of your family members may get an appreciation or recognition. There may be growth in the family or some family function for which you will be playing a major role as a responsible family member or as a sponsor for the function.

You will get some respite from the problems you have been facing for the last few months. You will have optimism and confidence in handling financial matters and making wise decisions related to money. You will be inclined to be generous and engage in charitable activities, supporting others in need.

After 18 May 2025, once Rahu transit to the Aquarius sign, you will find a lot of positivity which will help you to grow in social circles and friends' groups. You will make unconventional efforts to grow in business. You may find support from some old colleague who will help you to get a better job, start a new venture or in your professional efforts. Those who are in media, publication, writing or have soft skills will get the expected support. Those who are in the public domain may get an unexpected and sudden boost in their reputation. However, there may be problems in the acquisition of education and maintaining a love relationship.

For those who are expecting progeny, I advise them to consult the Doctor regularly. After 7 June 2025, when Mars transit to Leo sign and conjunct with Ketu, special attention needs to be given for progeny related issues or those who have conceived need to be extra cautious.

The period after 07 June 2025 to 28 July 2025 will be quite stressful for love relations. Due to anger issues or desire to dominate the love one can create a rift between two. Be submissive and avoid arrogance. Take care of your health regarding the digestion part. Medical attention may be required during this period.

Those who are unmarried are going to find a suitable proposal. That proposal may not be from their love relationship but more of an arranged marriage.

Period: 15 June to 15 July 2025

Planetary position on 15 June 2024, at the time Sun transits to Gemini will be as per the chart: -

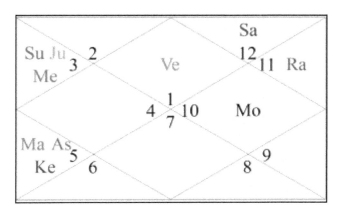

During this period, Mercury will enter Cancer on 22 June 2025, Venus enter Taurus on 29 June 2025. Saturn is going to be retrograde on 13 Jul 2025 in Pisces Sign. This retrogradation of 139 days is likely to affect all the signs especially signs which are aspected by Saturn.

In Leo sign, Ketu and Mars conjunct from 7 June to 28 July 2025. In Gemini, Jupiter and Venus conjunct from 26 Jul to 21 Aug 2025.

During this period, the Sun will transit in the third house and conjunct with Jupiter till 15 July 2025. This conjunction will give good results regarding the profession, short travels and siblings. Those who are involved in artistic or intellectual pursuits may find the period very favorable. During this period, you will have a boost in your confidence, improved communication, start a new venture, and improve relations with siblings. Here I would like to clarify one thing when we talk about opening a venture it may not be an industry or office to be opened but may be a new idea that you want to implement according to your capabilities. On the positive side, it can give a great boost to your career. Those who are in politics may find this a great time when they may be able to influence the Public.

Your confidence will soar, and you'll feel more optimistic about life. This positive outlook will make you eager to take on challenges and go after your goals. New opportunities will open, leading to growth in various aspects of your life. Your efforts may be recognized, and you could see success in your endeavours. People around you will look up to you for guidance and inspiration, and you might find yourself leading important projects, ideas or ventures.

You may be interested in learning and gathering information. You may feel intellectually curious and eager to explore new subjects and interests.

You may be required to travel a lot for business or adventure activities. You might feel the urge to get out and explore your immediate environment. If you're involved in writing, blogging, or other forms of communication, this period can be productive for such endeavours. You may be required to handle local errands, paperwork, or administrative tasks more efficiently. This is a period when networking and making new connections can be beneficial, both personally and professionally. Your focus may be on communication with siblings and other family members. It's a good time for reconnecting and resolving any communication issues. You may experience an increase in social activities and conversations with those around you.

The period seems promising with positive prospects in various aspects of your life. There may be gains in income, rise in position, overall happiness, recovery from disease, success in new ventures, association, and appreciation by the seniors. This period is associated with recognition by superiors, promotion and appreciation of the job. Your focus area will be your profession, colleagues, short travels, and communications. You may feel more decisive and able to make quick decisions, especially concerning everyday matters. It's a good time for reconnecting and resolving any communication issues

However, on the relationship front, the period can be quite stressful. Due to anger issues or a desire to dominate in relations, one can create a rift between the two. Be submissive and avoid arrogance. Take care of your health regarding the digestion part. Medical attention may be required during this period. The health of children can be an issue of concern. For those who are awaiting progeny, this period may not be positive and the person has to wait.

Saturn retrogradation from 13 July 2025 is likely to affect your relationship. Gains that you were expecting may not fructify or get delayed. You may find some health issues or pains reemerge during this retrogradation period.

Period: 16 July to 16 Aug 2025

Planetary position on 16 July 2024, at the time Sun transit to Cancer will be as per the chart: -

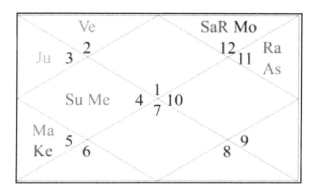

In this forthcoming period, Mercury becomes retrograde on 18 July 2025, Venus transit to Gemini on 26 July 2025 and Mars transit to Virgo on 28 July 2025. Mercury becomes direct in Cancer on 11 Aug 2025.

In Cancer, the Sun and Mercury conjunct from 16 Jul to 17 Aug 2025. In Gemini, Jupiter and Venus conjunct from 26 Jul to 21 Aug 2025

During this period, the Sun will transit in the fourth house which is the house of mother, comforts and luxuries of life, emotions and soft feelings. you will remain connected to your family members and home life. There might be a desire to spend more time at home or to engage in activities that involve your family. You may try to explore and understand your emotional needs and seek comfort and security within your family and close relationships.

After 18 July 2025, you may find that you are not able to decide on matters related to property. Renovation or dealing with the property may keep your mind in confusion. You get in a dilemma about how to react in family and social relationships, you may find situations beyond your control in relationships. If you are mid of a property deal, you may find some reversal. If you are planning to change jobs, you are advised to wait for some period and take a cautious approach till 11 Aug 2025. Avoid making any major investment decisions in stocks or business. There may be major fluctuation in stock markets from 18 July to 11 Aug 2025.

On 28 July 2025, Mars transits to Virgo and aspect the retrograde Saturn. Some health issues may emerge. Any minor accident or fight between some colleagues may happen. You will win over your enemies. If any litigation is in process, the result may be in your favour.

Those in a love relationship should remain docile. Better to keep patience and avoid anger or desire to dominate in a relationship. Be submissive and avoid arrogance. Take care of your health regarding the digestion part. Medical attention may be required during this period. Avoid any confrontation with your child. Take care of health issues of your child or brother, which may emerge.

Period: 17 Aug to 16 Sep 2025

Planetary position on 17 Aug 2024, at the time Sun transit to Leo will be as per the chart: -

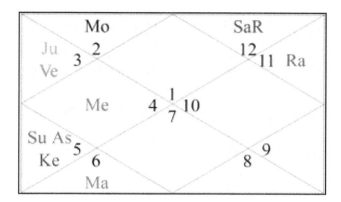

During this period, Venus transit to Cancer on 21 Aug 2025, Mercury to Leo on 30 Aug 2025, Mars in Libra on 13 Sep 2025 and Mercury in Virgo on 15 Sep 2025.

In Gemini, Jupiter and Venus conjunct from 26 Jul to 21 Aug 2025. Conjunction in Leo, Ketu and Sun from 17 Aug to 30 Aug 2025, in Cancer, Mercury and Venus from 21 Aug to 30 Aug 2025.

Sun and Ketu conjunction in the fifth house will bring positive transformations in one's life. It can lead to the individual earning name, fame and recognition due to their creative mind, hard work and dedicated work ethic. You may find time to engage in artistic or expressive activities, pursuing hobbies, artistic endeavours, and activities that bring joy. This may be due to the reason that during the adverse conditions on other fronts, you want to keep yourself occupied in your own world or get involved in activities that give you some relief. You might seek entertainment, engage in recreational activities, or attend social events that bring happiness. You may feel more adventurous and willing to step out of your comfort zone to pursue your passions. You may even go for an adventurous hike during this period. If you have a flair for performing or public speaking, then you may get an opportunity to showcase your talents and that may boost your confidence. You might be engaged in speculative ventures, such as investing or gambling. It's essential to exercise caution and not take excessive risks during this transit. You could get involved in spending time with children, being more involved in their lives, or considering matters related to parenting.

If you have a flair for performing or public speaking, then you may get an opportunity to showcase your talents and that may boost your confidence. You might be engaged in speculative ventures, such as investing or gambling. It's essential to exercise caution and not take excessive risks during this transit.

Those who are contemplating a career change might stumble upon a fitting job opportunity. On the health front, there could be a noticeable depletion of life force and energy due to health concerns affecting you or your family members, especially children. This might necessitate visits to the hospital to care for your loved ones and manage associated expenses.

For some individuals, this period might be related to matters of fertility, conception, or pregnancy. They must be careful for the entire duration of the transit of Ketu in the fifth house. The best way is not to ignore any health issues of your wife. Otherwise keep doing simple remedies for Ketu as feeding the ants, crows or handicapped people, worshiping lord Ganesha etc help to mitigate the negative effects of Ketu.

For students, this period can be quite positive and those who are looking to go abroad for higher studies may find success, but they will be struggling a lot for Visa. Those people who have the blessings of lord Ganesha may find success in their education and creative activities.

Period: 17 Sep to 17 Oct 2025

Planetary position on 17 Sep 2024, at the time Sun transit to Virgo will be as per the chart: -

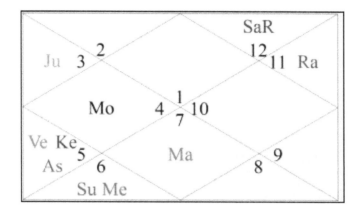

During the period, Mercury transits to Libra on 3 Oct 2025, and Venus in Virgo on 9 Oct 2025.

Conjunction In Leo, Ketu and Venus conjunct from 17 Sep to 9 Oct 2025. In Virgo, Sun and Mercury from 17 Sep to 3 Oct 2025, Sun and Venus from 9 Oct to 17 Oct 2025

This period can be quite positive as the Sun in the sixth house ensures your victory over enemies. Long pending issues, disputes or debts can be resolved. You will have success in financial matters. Those who are appearing in competitions may be successful. During this time, you could be quite busy with your work and managing your daily routine and responsibilities.

Any pending disputes will be solved during this period by your intelligence and strong willpower. There will be improvement in financial status. If any promotions, rewards or awards are pending, you will get them during this period. Your rapport with superiors will improve during this period. You will gain confidence, get success in new ventures and enjoy the luxuries of life.

Any health issues if troubling for long or since last month may be cured. You will be bestowed with good health, good earnings and success in new ventures. You may get involved with charitable activities. This is a good time to focus on personal growth and becoming better at various aspects of your life.

You may get the chance to showcase your leadership qualities by participating in important meetings, making crucial decisions, and guiding others. As a result, your public image and reputation are likely to improve, and people will admire and respect you for your achievements and contributions. If you've been seeking new job opportunities, promotions, upgrades, or rewards, this period holds the potential for success in these areas. Your appreciation may be recorded positive but may not be delivered.

During this period, practical tasks and responsibilities will require your attention. You may feel a strong desire to help others and be kind to them. It's an excellent opportunity to organize your life and create a structured daily routine. Simplifying and decluttering your living and working spaces might also be on your mind during this time.

On the family front, Venus Ketu conjunction and Mars in the seventh house is not quite positive and the native may find problems in love relations or with his life partner. The reason will be an ego clash or loss of trust in each other due to elevated sexual desires.

Period: 18 Oct to 16 Nov 2025

Planetary position on 17 Oct 2024, at the time Sun transit to Libra will be as per the chart: -

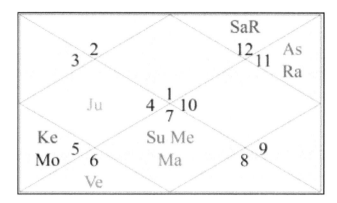

During this period, Jupiter transit to Cancer on 18 Oct 2025, Mercury in Scorpio on 24 Oct 2025, and Mars in Scorpio on 27 Oct 2025. On 10 Nov 2025, Mercury become retrograde in Scorpio and then on 11 Nov 2025, Jupiter become retrograde in Cancer.

Conjunction In Scorpio, Mars and Mercury from 27 Oct to 16 Nov 2025.

During this time, your focus will be on relationships, partnerships, marriage, and one-on-one connections. You'll likely pay more attention to your significant relationships, such as with your spouse, romantic partner, or close business associates. There will be increased interactions and activities with them. You might feel more assertive in your relationships and dominate in partnerships.

If you are married, there may be some problems in your married life. It's advised to be cautious and avoid unnecessary arguments or conflicts with your life partner during this time to prevent any trouble. Sun and Mars will be in transit in the seventh house till 27 Oct 2025. Two separatist planets in the seventh house and Venus in the sixth house are not a positive transit for married life. Having undue expectations from partner may create a rift so be practical and try to understand the problems of others. Those who tend to be cosy easily with opposite sex friends are advised to remain in social and oral norms.

Your social connections might be affected by your attitude, so be mindful of how you interact with others. Take care of the health of your parents and your life partner during this period.

Legal matters or negotiations with others may come into the picture more prominently, but the outcomes may not always align with your desires. It's important to find a balance between asserting your independence and the need for cooperation and compromise in your partnerships.

On the professional front and for your social status, you may grow and can have major gains in your profession. This is a positive time for career success, leadership, and positive social interactions. You will be ambitious and aggressive in your professional life but still tend to have a vast and diverse social network. You will be friendly, outgoing, and enjoy being part of various groups and communities. People will be drawn towards you due to your charismatic and confident personality. You will have ambitious goals and dreams which you want to achieve. However, to achieve success you must work hard and also remain grounded and humble.

After 27 Oct 2025, you should be cautious about any health issue. You have to be careful while driving the vehicle.

Period: 17 Nov to 15 Dec 2025

The planetary position on 16 Nov 2024, at the time Sun transit to Scorpio will be as per the chart: -

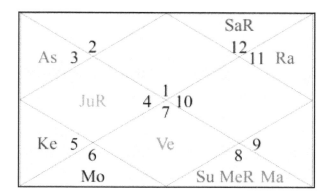

During this period, Mercury transits to Libra on 23 Nov 2025, Venus in Scorpio on 26 Nov 2025. Saturn becomes direct on 28 Nov 2025 in Pisces. Mercury becomes direct in Libra on 29 Nov 2025 and then enters Scorpio on 16 Dec 2025.

Conjunction, In Scorpio, Sun, Mars and Mercury from 16 Nov to 26 Nov 2025. In Scorpio Sun, Venus and Mars from 26 Nov to 29 Nov 2025, Sun, Venus, Mercury and Mars from 29 Nov to 16 Dec 2025.

Sun transit in the eighth house may bring some health issues. There could be a noticeable depletion of life force and energy due to health concerns affecting you or your family members, especially the parents of your or yours's life partner. This might necessitate visits to the hospital to care for your loved ones and manage associated expenses. The aspect of Jupiter is the saving grace and may provide major relief and help you with all problems. You can also consider that in times of crisis, guidance or help from some of your elder family members will be your savior.

You may become an introvert and would like to analyse the decisions taken in the past. It's a time for introspection and understanding your desires, fears, and motivations. it can signify a time of significant inner growth and personal evolution. There may be many financial ups and downs during this period. You may gain wealth from others or by management of wealth of others or through commission for any conducted deal or even after maturity of insurance policy.

You may be linked to the mystical, occult, and esoteric subjects and find yourself drawn to such matters or have experiences that encourage you to believe in occult studies or take guidance from any astrologer or palmist.

This period may bring situations or events that challenge you to confront and overcome deep-seated fears or issues which you have been avoiding since long.

During this period, you may be faced with opportunities or challenges regarding financial matters, such as inheritance, loans, debts, or joint ventures. Investments in stocks or mutual funds may be in a instable mode and you need to wait rather than get in a panic. Those having inheritance issues still have to wait for a positive outcome.

After 26 Nov 2025, there could be an increased focus on romantic interactions, and you may feel more playful and spontaneous in your relationships. You could get involved in spending time with children, being more involved in their lives, or considering matters related to parenting.

Period: 16 Dec to 31 Dec 2025

The planetary position on 16 Dec 2025, at the time Sun transit to Scorpio will be as per the chart: -

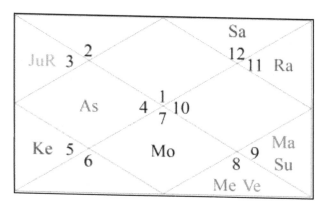

During this period, Venus transits to Sagittarius on 16 Dec 2025, and Mercury transits to Sagittarius on 29 Dec 2025.

In Sagittarius, Sun and Mars conjunct from 16 Dec to 20 Dec 2025, Sun, Mars and Venus from 20 Dec to 29 Dec 2025, Sun, Mars, Mercury and Venus from 25 Dec 2025 to 13 Jan 2026.

During this period, the Sun will be in transit in the ninth house, the house of religion, morality, higher education and father. Your focus area will be your parents, long travels, religious activities and legal issues.

You will remain energetic during this period. It is a favorable time to take a trip, embark on an adventure, or engage in activities that expand your knowledge and understanding of the world. You might feel motivated to study new subjects engage in activities that stimulate your intellectual curiosity or impart your higher education. If you're involved in the touring job, you may be required to visit long distances or even foreign places.

During this period, you can expect a lot of positivity and numerous opportunities coming your way. Your confidence will soar, and you'll feel more optimistic about life. This positive outlook will make you eager to take on challenges and go after your goals. Those in politics or positions of power and authority may find the period quite positive for them. New opportunities will open, leading to growth in various aspects of your life. Your efforts may be recognized, and you could see success in your endeavours. People around you will look up to you for guidance and inspiration, and you might find yourself leading important projects.

This is a positive period for students as they are successful. Your pursuit of spiritual matters and philosophical contemplation may lead you to travel and meet some religious people.

You may experience an increase in social activities and conversations with those around you. You will get happiness from brothers and sisters and even your children, however expectations from them may lead to stress. The health of siblings may be an issue of concern for you

However, you need to avoid arrogance with the seniors and your father. Your stubbornness and aggressive attitude can land you antagonizing the elders and superiors. There may be certain delays to the acquisition of the property which you are planning. Keep an eye on your father's health during this period and be prepared for possible disagreements with others.

Predictions Based on Moon Transit

The journey of Annual Horoscope 2025, began with the predictions based on transit of major planets and then shifted to Solar movement, which could forecast events monthly.

The effect during the entire month cannot be same as Moon which passes through each sign in 2 1/4 days and covers 12 Rasis roughly in 30 days from birth sign (Janma Rasi) has major effects on happening in our life. However further to bring at almost daily basis, we will be going through predictions based on Moon transit. How the day will be today based on Moon transit in a particular Nakshatra.

In the first part of this chapter, I will be going through the effects which you may observe in a span of 2 ¼ days. This will be based on Moon transit in a particular house of the chart. These predictions are generally quite accurate and help you to plan the activities.

In the second part of this chapter, I will be going further to period of each day of year 2025. You should consider these predictions while making any important activities.

Moon goes through a Rasi complete Zodiac which means that he will be good about 16 days in a month. The good results are not continuous but intermittent. During the same time the other planets give either good or bad results. Though it will not be humanly possible to give effects of other planets here, I will be covering the predictions based on Moon transit in a particular house only.

In essence, understanding the nuances of Moon transits in astrology will give you an idea of what is going on in life, but the details that are given can differ in your chart because of different natal chart. Every chart carries a different promise and dasha and Transit will deliver the promise as the event only.

You need to check the date and time given in table and events that may happen in that day. The charts given cover the dates of entire year when Moon transit over a particular house.

Moon in First House

Date From	Date to	Date From	Date to
07/01/2025 17:49	09/01/2025 20:46	03/02/2025 23:16	06/02/2025 02:15
03/03/2025 06:39	05/03/2025 08:12	30/03/2025 16:34	01/04/2025 16:30
27/04/2025 03:38	29/04/2025 02:53	24/05/2025 13:48	26/05/2025 13:40
20/06/2025 21:44	22/06/2025 23:03	18/07/2025 03:39	20/07/2025 06:11
14/08/2025 09:05	16/08/2025 11:43	10/09/2025 16:03	12/09/2025 17:30
08/10/2025 01:28	10/10/2025 01:23	04/11/2025 12:34	06/11/2025 11:46
01/12/2025 23:18	03/12/2025 23:14	29/12/2025 07:40	31/12/2025 09:23

This period promises comfort and luxury. You may purchase high-end items or vehicles and have opportunities to interact with people of higher status. Your good work may be appreciated by your seniors, leading to satisfaction with your performance and achieved results. It is a favorable time for progeny and learning Tantra and Mantras. Travel opportunities might arise, offering new learning experiences. You will enjoy good company, food, and other luxuries, and find satisfaction in family life, including sexual pleasure. A sense of contentment and self-assurance will often envelop you.

Financially, this period is favorable. You will easily recover dues and achieve your financial goals. Your married life will improve, enhancing your relationship with your spouse. It's a great time to enjoy with friends and acquaintances, particularly with the opposite sex. You and your family will experience good health without physical ailments. However, sometimes unstable thoughts may cause problems.

Moon in Second house

Date From	Date to		Date From	Date to
09/01/2025 20:46	11/01/2025 23:55		06/02/2025 02:15	08/02/2025 06:21
05/03/2025 08:12	07/03/2025 11:45		01/04/2025 16:30	03/04/2025 18:21
29/04/2025 02:53	01/05/2025 03:14		26/05/2025 13:40	28/05/2025 13:36
22/06/2025 23:03	24/06/2025 23:45		20/07/2025 06:11	22/07/2025 08:14
16/08/2025 11:43	18/08/2025 14:40		12/09/2025 17:30	14/09/2025 20:03
10/10/2025 01:23	12/10/2025 02:24		06/11/2025 11:46	08/11/2025 11:14
03/12/2025 23:14	05/12/2025 22:15		31/12/2025 09:23	02/01/2026 09:25

This period may bring certain challenges on the financial and professional fronts. You might face fears of punishment from the government, such as paying late fees for bills or traffic fines. Despite your best efforts, your seniors may not agree with your suggestions or be satisfied with your performance. Your colleagues might avoid you and fail to cooperate, leading to unwanted expenditures. It is crucial to avoid impulsive spending and risky investments during this time.

Disagreements and quarrels with your spouse and friends are likely, so it's best to avoid arguments in all areas of life. You may feel frustration and discontentment. Eye problems may arise, and it is advisable to avoid traveling. Meditation could help alleviate the mental and physical fatigue associated with this period.

Remember, these challenges will only last for a short time.

Moon in The Third House

Date From	Date to		Date From	Date to
11/01/2025 23:55	14/01/2025 04:19		08/02/2025 06:21	10/02/2025 11:56
07/03/2025 11:45	09/03/2025 17:45		03/04/2025 18:21	05/04/2025 23:25
01/05/2025 03:14	03/05/2025 06:36		28/05/2025 13:36	30/05/2025 15:42
24/06/2025 23:45	27/06/2025 01:39		22/07/2025 08:14	24/07/2025 10:59
18/08/2025 14:40	20/08/2025 18:35		14/09/2025 20:03	17/09/2025 00:28
12/10/2025 02:24	14/10/2025 05:58		08/11/2025 11:14	10/11/2025 13:03
05/12/2025 22:15	07/12/2025 22:38			

This period promises mental peace, happiness, comfort, and satisfaction from all sides. You may receive good news within the family and find time to spend with your children. Self-confidence will help you face life's challenges. Your spouse will be cooperative, enhancing your enjoyment of intimate moments. Your siblings will prosper and succeed, and all your endeavors will be successful. Financially, you will see money coming from multiple sources, and your relationships with your spouse, neighbors, and relatives, especially younger siblings, will be strong.

You will have the courage to overcome obstacles and foster stronger bonds with friends and siblings. Your health will improve, and you will achieve significant success in your profession, meeting your desired goals. Your work will be appreciated, recognized, and rewarded by your superiors. This period will also be very rewarding financially, allowing you to recover past dues and gain well in all financial ventures. It is a good time for short-distance travel.

Overall, you will be happy and satisfied with life, enjoying everything that comes your way.

Moon in the Fourth house

Date From	Date to		Date From	Date to
14/01/2025 04:19	16/01/2025 11:16		10/02/2025 11:56	12/02/2025 19:35
09/03/2025 17:45	12/03/2025 02:15		05/04/2025 23:25	08/04/2025 07:54
03/05/2025 06:36	05/05/2025 14:01		30/05/2025 15:42	01/06/2025 21:36
27/06/2025 01:39	29/06/2025 06:34		24/07/2025 10:59	26/07/2025 15:52
20/08/2025 18:35	23/08/2025 00:16		17/09/2025 00:28	19/09/2025 07:05
14/10/2025 05:58	16/10/2025 12:42		10/11/2025 13:03	12/11/2025 18:35
07/12/2025 22:38	10/12/2025 02:22			

There will be no peace at home. You will be in general unhappy and will not be able to enjoy due to mental or health issues. A sense of restlessness, grief, fear and doubt will prevail. Try your best to keep your cool and do not lose your mental balance. There will be lack of comforts and mental peace. If the body constitution is weak, stomach pain, dysentery, digestive disorders and chest problems may come up. Drive carefully as it is an accident prone period.

This will be a bad period for mother as she may suffer bad health. Expenditures will increase. You may find impediments in works. You must be very careful with your investment ventures as it is a period of losses.

Relations will be sore and there will be a lack of understanding. There will be trouble from relatives, especially the ones from your mother's side. Avoid clashes and hostility. Some of your relatives may suffer loss of wealth and this may cause grief to you.

The time is not suitable for travelling. If forced to travel take double care of your health and expenses.

Moon in the Fifth House

Date From	Date to		Date From	Date to
16/01/2025 11:16	18/01/2025 21:28		12/02/2025 19:35	15/02/2025 05:44
12/03/2025 02:15	14/03/2025 12:56		08/04/2025 07:54	10/04/2025 19:04
05/05/2025 14:01	08/05/2025 00:57		01/06/2025 21:36	04/06/2025 07:35
29/06/2025 06:34	01/07/2025 15:23		26/07/2025 15:52	29/07/2025 00:00
23/08/2025 00:16	25/08/2025 08:28		19/09/2025 07:05	21/09/2025 15:57
16/10/2025 12:42	18/10/2025 22:11		12/11/2025 18:35	15/11/2025 03:51
10/12/2025 02:22	12/12/2025 10:20			

During this period, issues concerning your children will take center stage. You will need to pay close attention to their health, emotions, and studies. Professionally, you will have to work harder to prove your competence and maintain your reputation. Meeting targets may be challenging due to various obstacles. If you are an investor or deal in financial markets, exercise caution.

Support from friends, colleagues, and even loved ones may be lacking. Be mindful of your food habits. Travel may present obstructions and risks of accidents, so take extra precautions. There will be wasteful expenditures, so take care of your belongings and avoid unnecessary spending.

Moon in the Sixth House

Date From	Date to		Date From	Date to
18/01/2025 21:28	21/01/2025 10:03		15/02/2025 05:44	17/02/2025 18:02
14/03/2025 12:56	17/03/2025 01:15		10/04/2025 19:04	13/04/2025 07:38
08/05/2025 00:57	10/05/2025 13:42		04/06/2025 07:35	06/06/2025 20:06
01/07/2025 15:23	04/07/2025 03:19		29/07/2025 00:00	31/07/2025 11:15
25/08/2025 08:28	27/08/2025 19:21		21/09/2025 15:57	24/09/2025 02:55
18/10/2025 22:11	21/10/2025 09:36		15/11/2025 03:51	17/11/2025 15:35
12/12/2025 10:20	14/12/2025 21:41			

The period will be excellent as you will be able to handle your affairs in a confident manner. There will be all round improvement. There will be comforts during travel. You may get an opportunity to connect and liaise with new friends especially females and will enjoy their company.

You will be in an energetic and enthusiastic mood and will work comfortably at a fast pace. You will get victory over your enemies and competitors and will be successful in finishing the stuck-up undertakings. You will get good recognition and rewards from the bosses. Financially it is a very good period of gains and investments will yield good returns.

This period brings with it a ray of hope and auspicious outcomes. Success in efforts again, domestic harmony, and victory over adversaries is indicated during this period, instilling a sense of confidence and stability in natives.

Moon in the Seventh House

Date From	Date to	Date From	Date to
21/01/2025 10:03	23/01/2025 22:32	17/02/2025 18:02	20/02/2025 06:49
17/03/2025 01:15	19/03/2025 14:06	13/04/2025 07:38	15/04/2025 20:26
10/05/2025 13:42	13/05/2025 02:27	06/06/2025 20:06	09/06/2025 08:50
04/07/2025 03:19	06/07/2025 16:00	31/07/2025 11:15	02/08/2025 23:52
27/08/2025 19:21	30/08/2025 07:52	24/09/2025 02:55	26/09/2025 15:23
21/10/2025 09:36	23/10/2025 22:05	17/11/2025 15:35	20/11/2025 04:13
14/12/2025 21:41	17/12/2025 10:26		

This period will be excellent, allowing you to handle your affairs with confidence. You will see overall improvement and comfort, especially during travel. You will have opportunities to meet and connect with new friends, particularly women, and will enjoy their company.

You will feel energetic and enthusiastic, working quickly and comfortably. You will defeat your enemies and competitors, and successfully finish any pending tasks. Your efforts will be recognized and rewarded by your bosses. Financially, this is a very good time, with gains and profitable returns on investments.

This period brings hope and positive outcomes. You will succeed in your efforts, enjoy harmony at home, and overcome adversaries, leading to confidence and stability.

Moon in the Eighth house

Date From	Date to	Date From	Date to
23/01/2025 22:32	26/01/2025 08:26	20/02/2025 06:49	22/02/2025 17:40
19/03/2025 14:06	22/03/2025 01:45	15/04/2025 20:26	18/04/2025 08:20
13/05/2025 02:27	15/05/2025 14:07	09/06/2025 08:50	11/06/2025 20:10
06/07/2025 16:00	09/07/2025 03:15	02/08/2025 23:52	05/08/2025 11:22
30/08/2025 07:52	01/09/2025 19:55	26/09/2025 15:23	29/09/2025 03:54
23/10/2025 22:05	26/10/2025 10:46	20/11/2025 04:13	22/11/2025 16:46
17/12/2025 10:26	19/12/2025 22:51		

This period brings lot of problems, obstacles and sufferings. There will be many obstacles in your path at your workplace. Avoid conflicts and disagreements with your seniors. Do not indulge in and secret dealings or scheming. Your enemies will increase and will give you troubles. Money will not come on time. Avoid all investments as it is a very bad period and possibility of losses is very strong.

The mind is diverted to follow the wrong practices. Due to pressure from spouse, you may get in enmity with others. There will be quarrels and disagreements at home. Married life will suffer. You may be thinking of evil about others and that attitude may result in hardship for you.

Unnecessary fear and anxiety, a sense of loss and gloom will prevail. A very bad time for health. Be careful while crossing the road and avoid all games, sports and activities involving physical risk. Avoid travelling as it is a very bad period for accidents and calamities.

Moon in the Ninth House

Date From	Date to		Date From	Date to
26/01/2025 08:26	28/01/2025 14:51		22/02/2025 17:40	25/02/2025 00:55
22/03/2025 01:45	24/03/2025 10:24		18/04/2025 08:20	20/04/2025 18:04
15/05/2025 14:07	18/05/2025 00:03		11/06/2025 20:10	14/06/2025 05:38
09/07/2025 03:15	11/07/2025 12:08		05/08/2025 11:22	07/08/2025 20:11
01/09/2025 19:55	04/09/2025 05:21		29/09/2025 03:54	01/10/2025 14:27
26/10/2025 10:46	28/10/2025 22:14		22/11/2025 16:46	25/11/2025 04:26
19/12/2025 22:51	22/12/2025 10:06			

This period will bring positive results in all respects. You may feel drawn to spirituality and wish to visit a religious place. The time will be good for your wife and children, and you might experience a heightened temptation towards sex. Your humanitarian and charitable activities will be recognized. You will enjoy luxuries and travel. However, it is important to avoid disagreements or fights with your father.

Moon in the Tenth house

Date From	Date to		Date From	Date to
01/01/2025 06:01	03/01/2025 10:47		28/01/2025 14:51	30/01/2025 18:34
25/02/2025 00:55	27/02/2025 04:36		24/03/2025 10:24	26/03/2025 15:14
20/04/2025 18:04	23/04/2025 00:31		18/05/2025 00:03	20/05/2025 07:35
14/06/2025 05:38	16/06/2025 13:09		11/07/2025 12:08	13/07/2025 18:53
07/08/2025 20:11	10/08/2025 02:11		04/09/2025 05:21	06/09/2025 11:21
01/10/2025 14:27	03/10/2025 21:27		28/10/2025 22:14	31/10/2025 06:48
25/11/2025 04:26	27/11/2025 14:07		22/12/2025 10:06	24/12/2025 19:46

This is a very good time professionally. Your work will yield desirable results and earn the appreciation of your bosses. A promotion or honor is likely. Financially, this period is rewarding, making it an excellent time to start new projects. Money will come when needed, and investments will yield good returns.

Your family life will be happy and contented, with good conjugal bliss and a satisfying social life. You will gain a good reputation and respect in society. You may also need to travel for professional reasons.

Moon in the Eleventh House

Date From	Date to		Date From	Date to
03/01/2025 10:47	05/01/2025 14:34		30/01/2025 18:34	01/02/2025 20:58
27/02/2025 04:36	01/03/2025 05:57		26/03/2025 15:14	28/03/2025 16:47
23/04/2025 00:31	25/04/2025 03:25		20/05/2025 07:35	22/05/2025 12:08
16/06/2025 13:09	18/06/2025 18:35		13/07/2025 18:53	15/07/2025 23:58
10/08/2025 02:11	12/08/2025 06:10		06/09/2025 11:21	08/09/2025 14:29
03/10/2025 21:27	06/10/2025 00:45		31/10/2025 06:48	02/11/2025 11:27
27/11/2025 14:07	29/11/2025 20:33		24/12/2025 19:46	27/12/2025 03:10

During this period, you will experience good progress at work and will be supported by your friends, spouse, and seniors. Your bosses will respect and appreciate your efforts, and you may receive rewards. It's an excellent time for financial gains, with a boost in income and the ability to recover old dues. All financial investments will be fruitful, yielding very good returns.

On a personal level, this period brings happiness, joy, and a harmonious conjugal life. Your children will be affectionate and bring you happiness. You will make new friends and enjoy the company of the opposite sex. Your social life will be active with family reunions and gatherings with friends. Eligible individuals may even meet their future spouse.

You will enjoy worldly comforts, and your mood will be upbeat with a sense of delight and happiness. This is an auspicious time for travel, especially long-distance air travel, which will be fruitful and enjoyable.

Moon in the Twelfth House

Date From	Date to		Date From	Date to
05/01/2025 14:34	07/01/2025 17:49		01/02/2025 20:58	03/02/2025 23:16
01/03/2025 05:57	03/03/2025 06:39		28/03/2025 16:47	30/03/2025 16:34
25/04/2025 03:25	27/04/2025 03:38		22/05/2025 12:08	24/05/2025 13:48
18/06/2025 18:35	20/06/2025 21:44		15/07/2025 23:58	18/07/2025 03:39
12/08/2025 06:10	14/08/2025 09:05		08/09/2025 14:29	10/09/2025 16:03
06/10/2025 00:45	08/10/2025 01:28		02/11/2025 11:27	04/11/2025 12:34
29/11/2025 20:33	01/12/2025 23:18		27/12/2025 03:10	29/12/2025 07:40

During this period, you may face struggles and encounter obstacles. Your mind will be troubled by worries and fears, making it difficult to achieve desired targets despite your hard work. Your efforts may go unappreciated by your seniors. It's crucial to avoid underhand dealings and illegal activities. Instead of seeking progress and prosperity, focus on damage control to preserve your mental, physical, and financial resources.

There will be increased expenditure and insufficient income, leading to financial losses in various ways. Avoid all financial investments and transactions as this is a period prone to losses.

On a personal level, avoid arguments and conflicts with your spouse and relatives. Love and marital life may face challenges during this time. Avoid unnecessary travels as they may not be fruitful.

Your mental peace will be disturbed, and you may feel uneasy. However, you may find friendship with individuals outside your usual circle.

Day Wise Predictions

After going through the predictions for 2 ¼ days, I would like to cover predictions for each day in the year 2025. How will be the day today. How will be my mood, progress, health, finances for the day. I will be covering the daily predictions based on the transit of Moon over the Nakshatras. Since, I cannot differentiate the Sign based predictions with Nakshatra based events so you require to check your Nakshatra of Moon.

Moon will transit through the same nakshatras after every 27 days but you don't see repetition of events in your life after every 27 days. That will be due to other factors as Dasha, Antar Dahsa and planetary position of other planets. However, the general effects will remain on the same pattern.

How to Check the Daily Predictions

The simple mean is to check Moon Nakshatra from your birth chart or check the degrees of your Moon in that particular sign. If the Moon falls in 0 degree to 13.20 degree, then take the Symbol X. If the Moon falls in degree 13.20 to 26.40 degrees, then Y and if Moon falls in 26.40 degree to 30 degree, then Z. In case of Aries sign, it will be Ashwini (X), Bharani (Y)

Foe example, if Moon is in Aries sign in Ashwini Nakshtra or from 0 degree to 13.20 degree, then use value X. If Moon in Aries sign, Bharani Nakshatra or from degrees 13.20 to 26.40 degrees then value Y. If Moon in Krittika Nakshatra or 26.40 degree to 30 degrees then value Z.

Further for the timelines, I have given Moon transit in each Nakshatra for the entire year 2025. You have to check the sequence in front of date from the chart below as per your Birth Nakshatra and read the results given below in heading "Result of Moon Transit as per tara Bala". Let us say your Birth Nakshatra is Ashwini and you want to check for date 15 Mar 2025. Since Ashwini is the first Nakshtra of Aries sign then it is X. Date 15 Mar 2025 will fall in span of Ser No 46. It is No 8 Result for Ashwini (X), No7 for Bharani (Y) and No 6 for Krittika (Z).

So I will go to Result sequence at "Result of Moon Transit as per Tara Bala" For Ashwini (X) , it will be "A good period with happiness, companionship, support from friends, gains through cooperation, and support." For Bharani Nakshtra(Y) it will be "A struggle period with inauspicious results, obstacles, dangers, severe misfortunes, troubles, illness, or loss".

Similarly, to check the day prediction, you may choose the day, your Nakshtra and Result sequence No. Check result from the "Result of Moon Transit as per Tara Bala".

Moon Transit in Nakshatra: 2025

Ser	Nk	Date Entry	Date Exit	X	Y	Z
1	21	01/01/2025 00:03	01/01/2025 23:45	3	2	1
2	22	01/01/2025 23:45	02/01/2025 23:10	4	3	2
3	23	02/01/2025 23:10	03/01/2025 22:21	5	4	3
4	24	03/01/2025 22:21	04/01/2025 21:23	6	5	4
5	25	04/01/2025 21:23	05/01/2025 20:17	7	6	5
6	26	05/01/2025 20:17	06/01/2025 19:06	8	7	6
7	27	06/01/2025 19:06	07/01/2025 17:49	9	8	7
8	1	07/01/2025 17:49	08/01/2025 16:29	1	9	8
9	2	08/01/2025 16:29	09/01/2025 15:06	2	1	9
10	3	09/01/2025 15:06	10/01/2025 13:45	4	2	1
11	4	10/01/2025 13:45	11/01/2025 12:29	5	4	2
12	5	11/01/2025 12:29	12/01/2025 11:24	6	5	4
13	6	12/01/2025 11:24	13/01/2025 10:37	7	6	5
14	7	13/01/2025 10:37	14/01/2025 10:16	8	7	6
15	8	14/01/2025 10:16	15/01/2025 10:27	9	8	7
16	9	15/01/2025 10:27	16/01/2025 11:16	1	9	8
17	10	16/01/2025 11:16	17/01/2025 12:44	2	1	9
18	11	17/01/2025 12:44	18/01/2025 14:51	4	2	1
19	12	18/01/2025 14:51	19/01/2025 17:29	5	4	2
20	13	19/01/2025 17:29	20/01/2025 20:29	6	5	4
21	14	20/01/2025 20:29	21/01/2025 23:36	7	6	5
22	15	21/01/2025 23:36	23/01/2025 02:34	8	7	6
23	16	23/01/2025 02:34	24/01/2025 05:08	9	8	7
24	17	24/01/2025 05:08	25/01/2025 07:07	1	9	8
25	18	25/01/2025 07:07	26/01/2025 08:25	2	1	9
26	19	26/01/2025 08:25	27/01/2025 09:01	4	2	1
27	20	27/01/2025 09:01	28/01/2025 08:58	5	4	2
28	21	28/01/2025 08:58	29/01/2025 08:20	6	5	4
29	22	29/01/2025 08:20	30/01/2025 07:14	7	6	5
30	23	30/01/2025 07:14	31/01/2025 05:50	8	7	6

Ser	Nk	Date Entry	Date Exit	X	Y	Z
31	24	31/01/2025 05:50	01/02/2025 04:14	9	8	7
32	25	01/02/2025 04:14	02/02/2025 02:32	1	9	8
33	26	02/02/2025 02:32	03/02/2025 00:51	2	1	9
34	27	03/02/2025 00:51	03/02/2025 23:16	4	2	1
35	1	03/02/2025 23:16	04/02/2025 21:49	5	4	2
36	2	04/02/2025 21:49	05/02/2025 20:32	6	5	4
37	3	05/02/2025 20:32	06/02/2025 19:29	7	6	5
38	4	06/02/2025 19:29	07/02/2025 18:39	8	7	6
39	5	07/02/2025 18:39	08/02/2025 18:06	9	8	7
40	6	08/02/2025 18:06	09/02/2025 17:52	1	9	8
41	7	09/02/2025 17:52	10/02/2025 18:00	2	1	9
42	8	10/02/2025 18:00	11/02/2025 18:33	4	2	1
43	9	11/02/2025 18:33	12/02/2025 19:35	5	4	2
44	10	12/02/2025 19:35	13/02/2025 21:06	6	5	4
45	11	13/02/2025 21:06	14/02/2025 23:09	7	6	5
46	12	14/02/2025 23:09	16/02/2025 01:39	8	7	6
47	13	16/02/2025 01:39	17/02/2025 04:31	9	8	7
48	14	17/02/2025 04:31	18/02/2025 07:35	1	9	8
49	15	18/02/2025 07:35	19/02/2025 10:39	2	1	9
50	16	19/02/2025 10:39	20/02/2025 13:30	4	2	1
51	17	20/02/2025 13:30	21/02/2025 15:53	5	4	2
52	18	21/02/2025 15:53	22/02/2025 17:40	6	5	4
53	19	22/02/2025 17:40	23/02/2025 18:42	7	6	5
54	20	23/02/2025 18:42	24/02/2025 18:58	8	7	6
55	21	24/02/2025 18:58	25/02/2025 18:30	9	8	7
56	22	25/02/2025 18:30	26/02/2025 17:23	1	9	8
57	23	26/02/2025 17:23	27/02/2025 15:43	2	1	9
58	24	27/02/2025 15:43	28/02/2025 13:40	4	2	1
59	25	28/02/2025 13:40	01/03/2025 11:22	5	4	2
60	26	01/03/2025 11:22	02/03/2025 08:59	6	5	4

61 27 02/03/2025 08:59 03/03/2025 06:38 7 6 5

Ser	Nk	Date Entry	Date Exit	X	Y	Z
62	1	03/03/2025 06:38	04/03/2025 04:29	8	7	6
63	2	04/03/2025 04:29	05/03/2025 02:37	9	8	7
64	3	05/03/2025 02:37	06/03/2025 01:08	1	9	8
65	4	06/03/2025 01:08	07/03/2025 00:05	2	1	9
66	5	07/03/2025 00:05	07/03/2025 23:31	4	2	1
67	6	07/03/2025 23:31	08/03/2025 23:28	5	4	2
68	7	08/03/2025 23:28	09/03/2025 23:54	6	5	4
69	8	09/03/2025 23:54	11/03/2025 00:51	7	6	5
70	9	11/03/2025 00:51	12/03/2025 02:15	8	7	6
71	10	12/03/2025 02:15	13/03/2025 04:05	9	8	7
72	11	13/03/2025 04:05	14/03/2025 06:19	1	9	8
73	12	14/03/2025 06:19	15/03/2025 08:53	2	1	9
74	13	15/03/2025 08:53	16/03/2025 11:45	4	2	1
75	14	16/03/2025 11:45	17/03/2025 14:46	5	4	2
76	15	17/03/2025 14:46	18/03/2025 17:51	6	5	4
77	16	18/03/2025 17:51	19/03/2025 20:49	7	6	5
78	17	19/03/2025 20:49	20/03/2025 23:31	8	7	6
79	18	20/03/2025 23:31	22/03/2025 01:45	9	8	7
80	19	22/03/2025 01:45	23/03/2025 03:23	1	9	8
81	20	23/03/2025 03:23	24/03/2025 04:18	2	1	9
82	21	24/03/2025 04:18	25/03/2025 04:26	4	2	1
83	22	25/03/2025 04:26	26/03/2025 03:49	5	4	2
84	23	26/03/2025 03:49	27/03/2025 02:29	6	5	4
85	24	27/03/2025 02:29	28/03/2025 00:33	7	6	5
86	25	28/03/2025 00:33	28/03/2025 22:09	8	7	6
87	26	28/03/2025 22:09	29/03/2025 19:26	9	8	7
88	27	29/03/2025 19:26	30/03/2025 16:34	1	9	8
89	1	30/03/2025 16:34	31/03/2025 13:44	2	1	9
90	2	31/03/2025 13:44	01/04/2025 11:06	4	2	1

Ser	Nk	Date Entry	Date Exit	X	Y	Z
91	3	01/04/2025 11:06	02/04/2025 08:49	5	4	2
92	4	02/04/2025 08:49	03/04/2025 07:02	6	5	4
93	5	03/04/2025 07:02	04/04/2025 05:50	7	6	5
94	6	04/04/2025 05:50	05/04/2025 05:20	8	7	6
95	7	05/04/2025 05:20	06/04/2025 05:31	9	8	7
96	8	06/04/2025 05:31	07/04/2025 06:24	1	9	8
97	9	07/04/2025 06:24	08/04/2025 07:54	2	1	9
98	10	08/04/2025 07:54	09/04/2025 09:56	4	2	1
99	11	09/04/2025 09:56	10/04/2025 12:24	5	4	2
100	12	10/04/2025 12:24	11/04/2025 15:10	6	5	4
101	13	11/04/2025 15:10	12/04/2025 18:07	7	6	5
102	14	12/04/2025 18:07	13/04/2025 21:10	8	7	6
103	15	13/04/2025 21:10	15/04/2025 00:13	9	8	7
104	16	15/04/2025 00:13	16/04/2025 03:10	1	9	8
105	17	16/04/2025 03:10	17/04/2025 05:54	2	1	9
106	18	17/04/2025 05:54	18/04/2025 08:20	4	2	1
107	19	18/04/2025 08:20	19/04/2025 10:20	5	4	2
108	20	19/04/2025 10:20	20/04/2025 11:48	6	5	4
109	21	20/04/2025 11:48	21/04/2025 12:36	7	6	5
110	22	21/04/2025 12:36	22/04/2025 12:43	8	7	6
111	23	22/04/2025 12:43	23/04/2025 12:07	9	8	7
112	24	23/04/2025 12:07	24/04/2025 10:49	1	9	8
113	25	24/04/2025 10:49	25/04/2025 08:53	2	1	9
114	26	25/04/2025 08:53	26/04/2025 06:27	4	2	1
115	27	26/04/2025 06:27	27/04/2025 03:38	5	4	2
116	1	27/04/2025 03:38	28/04/2025 00:38	6	5	4
117	2	28/04/2025 00:38	28/04/2025 21:37	7	6	5
118	3	28/04/2025 21:37	29/04/2025 18:46	8	7	6
119	4	29/04/2025 18:46	30/04/2025 16:17	9	8	7
120	5	30/04/2025 16:17	01/05/2025 14:20	1	9	8

Ser	Nk	Date Entry	Date Exit	X	Y	Z
121	6	01/05/2025 14:20	02/05/2025 13:03	2	1	9
122	7	02/05/2025 13:03	03/05/2025 12:33	4	2	1
123	8	03/05/2025 12:33	04/05/2025 12:53	5	4	2
124	9	04/05/2025 12:53	05/05/2025 14:01	6	5	4
125	10	05/05/2025 14:01	06/05/2025 15:51	7	6	5
126	11	06/05/2025 15:51	07/05/2025 18:16	8	7	6
127	12	07/05/2025 18:16	08/05/2025 21:06	9	8	7
128	13	08/05/2025 21:06	10/05/2025 00:08	1	9	8
129	14	10/05/2025 00:08	11/05/2025 03:15	2	1	9
130	15	11/05/2025 03:15	12/05/2025 06:17	4	2	1
131	16	12/05/2025 06:17	13/05/2025 09:09	5	4	2
132	17	13/05/2025 09:09	14/05/2025 11:46	6	5	4
133	18	14/05/2025 11:46	15/05/2025 14:07	7	6	5
134	19	15/05/2025 14:07	16/05/2025 16:07	8	7	6
135	20	16/05/2025 16:07	17/05/2025 17:43	9	8	7
136	21	17/05/2025 17:43	18/05/2025 18:52	1	9	8
137	22	18/05/2025 18:52	19/05/2025 19:29	2	1	9
138	23	19/05/2025 19:29	20/05/2025 19:31	4	2	1
139	24	20/05/2025 19:31	21/05/2025 18:57	5	4	2
140	25	21/05/2025 18:57	22/05/2025 17:47	6	5	4
141	26	22/05/2025 17:47	23/05/2025 16:02	7	6	5
142	27	23/05/2025 16:02	24/05/2025 13:48	8	7	6
143	1	24/05/2025 13:48	25/05/2025 11:12	9	8	7
144	2	25/05/2025 11:12	26/05/2025 08:23	1	9	8
145	3	26/05/2025 08:23	27/05/2025 05:32	2	1	9
146	4	27/05/2025 05:32	28/05/2025 02:50	4	2	1
147	5	28/05/2025 02:50	29/05/2025 00:28	5	4	2
148	6	29/05/2025 00:28	29/05/2025 22:38	6	5	4
149	7	29/05/2025 22:38	30/05/2025 21:28	7	6	5
150	8	30/05/2025 21:28	31/05/2025 21:07	8	7	6

Ser	Nk	Date Entry	Date Exit	X	Y	Z
151	9	31/05/2025 21:07	01/06/2025 21:36	9	8	7
152	10	01/06/2025 21:36	02/06/2025 22:55	1	9	8
153	11	02/06/2025 22:55	04/06/2025 00:58	2	1	9
154	12	04/06/2025 00:58	05/06/2025 03:35	4	2	1
155	13	05/06/2025 03:35	06/06/2025 06:33	5	4	2
156	14	06/06/2025 06:33	07/06/2025 09:39	6	5	4
157	15	07/06/2025 09:39	08/06/2025 12:41	7	6	5
158	16	08/06/2025 12:41	09/06/2025 15:30	8	7	6
159	17	09/06/2025 15:30	10/06/2025 18:01	9	8	7
160	18	10/06/2025 18:01	11/06/2025 20:10	1	9	8
161	19	11/06/2025 20:10	12/06/2025 21:56	2	1	9
162	20	12/06/2025 21:56	13/06/2025 23:20	4	2	1
163	21	13/06/2025 23:20	15/06/2025 00:21	5	4	2
164	22	15/06/2025 00:21	16/06/2025 00:59	6	5	4
165	23	16/06/2025 00:59	17/06/2025 01:13	7	6	5
166	24	17/06/2025 01:13	18/06/2025 01:01	8	7	6
167	25	18/06/2025 01:01	19/06/2025 00:22	9	8	7
168	26	19/06/2025 00:22	19/06/2025 23:16	1	9	8
169	27	19/06/2025 23:16	20/06/2025 21:44	2	1	9
170	1	20/06/2025 21:44	21/06/2025 19:49	4	2	1
171	2	21/06/2025 19:49	22/06/2025 17:38	5	4	2
172	3	22/06/2025 17:38	23/06/2025 15:16	6	5	4
173	4	23/06/2025 15:16	24/06/2025 12:53	7	6	5
174	5	24/06/2025 12:53	25/06/2025 10:40	8	7	6
175	6	25/06/2025 10:40	26/06/2025 08:46	9	8	7
176	7	26/06/2025 08:46	27/06/2025 07:21	1	9	8
177	8	27/06/2025 07:21	28/06/2025 06:35	2	1	9
178	9	28/06/2025 06:35	29/06/2025 06:33	4	2	1
179	10	29/06/2025 06:33	30/06/2025 07:20	5	4	2
180	11	30/06/2025 07:20	01/07/2025 08:53	6	5	4

Ser	Nk	Date Entry	Date Exit	X	Y	Z
181	12	01/07/2025 08:53	02/07/2025 11:07	7	6	5
182	13	02/07/2025 11:07	03/07/2025 13:50	8	7	6
183	14	03/07/2025 13:50	04/07/2025 16:49	9	8	7
184	15	04/07/2025 16:49	05/07/2025 19:51	1	9	8
185	16	05/07/2025 19:51	06/07/2025 22:41	2	1	9
186	17	06/07/2025 22:41	08/07/2025 01:11	4	2	1
187	18	08/07/2025 01:11	09/07/2025 03:14	5	4	2
188	19	09/07/2025 03:14	10/07/2025 04:49	6	5	4
189	20	10/07/2025 04:49	11/07/2025 05:55	7	6	5
190	21	11/07/2025 05:55	12/07/2025 06:35	8	7	6
191	22	12/07/2025 06:35	13/07/2025 06:52	9	8	7
192	23	13/07/2025 06:52	14/07/2025 06:48	1	9	8
193	24	14/07/2025 06:48	15/07/2025 06:25	2	1	9
194	25	15/07/2025 06:25	16/07/2025 05:46	4	2	1
195	26	16/07/2025 05:46	17/07/2025 04:50	5	4	2
196	27	17/07/2025 04:50	18/07/2025 03:38	6	5	4
197	1	18/07/2025 03:38	19/07/2025 02:13	7	6	5
198	2	19/07/2025 02:13	20/07/2025 00:37	8	7	6
199	3	20/07/2025 00:37	20/07/2025 22:52	9	8	7
200	4	20/07/2025 22:52	21/07/2025 21:06	1	9	8
201	5	21/07/2025 21:06	22/07/2025 19:24	2	1	9
202	6	22/07/2025 19:24	23/07/2025 17:54	4	2	1
203	7	23/07/2025 17:54	24/07/2025 16:43	5	4	2
204	8	24/07/2025 16:43	25/07/2025 16:00	6	5	4
205	9	25/07/2025 16:00	26/07/2025 15:51	7	6	5
206	10	26/07/2025 15:51	27/07/2025 16:22	8	7	6
207	11	27/07/2025 16:22	28/07/2025 17:35	9	8	7
208	12	28/07/2025 17:35	29/07/2025 19:27	1	9	8
209	13	29/07/2025 19:27	30/07/2025 21:52	2	1	9
210	14	30/07/2025 21:52	01/08/2025 00:41	4	2	1

Ser	Nk	Date Entry	Date Exit	X	Y	Z
211	15	01/08/2025 00:41	02/08/2025 03:40	5	4	2
212	16	02/08/2025 03:40	03/08/2025 06:34	6	5	4
213	17	03/08/2025 06:34	04/08/2025 09:12	7	6	5
214	18	04/08/2025 09:12	05/08/2025 11:22	8	7	6
215	19	05/08/2025 11:22	06/08/2025 12:59	9	8	7
216	20	06/08/2025 12:59	07/08/2025 14:01	1	9	8
217	21	07/08/2025 14:01	08/08/2025 14:27	2	1	9
218	22	08/08/2025 14:27	09/08/2025 14:23	4	2	1
219	23	09/08/2025 14:23	10/08/2025 13:52	5	4	2
220	24	10/08/2025 13:52	11/08/2025 12:59	6	5	4
221	25	11/08/2025 12:59	12/08/2025 11:51	7	6	5
222	26	12/08/2025 11:51	13/08/2025 10:32	8	7	6
223	27	13/08/2025 10:32	14/08/2025 09:05	9	8	7
224	1	14/08/2025 09:05	15/08/2025 07:35	1	9	8
225	2	15/08/2025 07:35	16/08/2025 06:05	2	1	9
226	3	16/08/2025 06:05	17/08/2025 04:38	4	2	1
227	4	17/08/2025 04:38	18/08/2025 03:17	5	4	2
228	5	18/08/2025 03:17	19/08/2025 02:05	6	5	4
229	6	19/08/2025 02:05	20/08/2025 01:07	7	6	5
230	7	20/08/2025 01:07	21/08/2025 00:26	8	7	6
231	8	21/08/2025 00:26	22/08/2025 00:08	9	8	7
232	9	22/08/2025 00:08	23/08/2025 00:16	1	9	8
233	10	23/08/2025 00:16	24/08/2025 00:54	2	1	9
234	11	24/08/2025 00:54	25/08/2025 02:05	4	2	1
235	12	25/08/2025 02:05	26/08/2025 03:49	5	4	2
236	13	26/08/2025 03:49	27/08/2025 06:04	6	5	4
237	14	27/08/2025 06:04	28/08/2025 08:43	7	6	5
238	15	28/08/2025 08:43	29/08/2025 11:38	8	7	6
239	16	29/08/2025 11:38	30/08/2025 14:37	9	8	7
240	17	30/08/2025 14:37	31/08/2025 17:26	1	9	8

Ser	Nk	Date Entry	Date Exit	X	Y	Z
241	18	31/08/2025 17:26	01/09/2025 19:54	2	1	9
242	19	01/09/2025 19:54	02/09/2025 21:50	4	2	1
243	20	02/09/2025 21:50	03/09/2025 23:08	5	4	2
244	21	03/09/2025 23:08	04/09/2025 23:43	6	5	4
245	22	04/09/2025 23:43	05/09/2025 23:38	7	6	5
246	23	05/09/2025 23:38	06/09/2025 22:55	8	7	6
247	24	06/09/2025 22:55	07/09/2025 21:40	9	8	7
248	25	07/09/2025 21:40	08/09/2025 20:02	1	9	8
249	26	08/09/2025 20:02	09/09/2025 18:06	2	1	9
250	27	09/09/2025 18:06	10/09/2025 16:02	4	2	1
251	1	10/09/2025 16:02	11/09/2025 13:57	5	4	2
252	2	11/09/2025 13:57	12/09/2025 11:58	6	5	4
253	3	12/09/2025 11:58	13/09/2025 10:11	7	6	5
254	4	13/09/2025 10:11	14/09/2025 08:40	8	7	6
255	5	14/09/2025 08:40	15/09/2025 07:31	9	8	7
256	6	15/09/2025 07:31	16/09/2025 06:45	1	9	8
257	7	16/09/2025 06:45	17/09/2025 06:25	2	1	9
258	8	17/09/2025 06:25	18/09/2025 06:31	4	2	1
259	9	18/09/2025 06:31	19/09/2025 07:05	5	4	2
260	10	19/09/2025 07:05	20/09/2025 08:05	6	5	4
261	11	20/09/2025 08:05	21/09/2025 09:31	7	6	5
262	12	21/09/2025 09:31	22/09/2025 11:23	8	7	6
263	13	22/09/2025 11:23	23/09/2025 13:39	9	8	7
264	14	23/09/2025 13:39	24/09/2025 16:16	1	9	8
265	15	24/09/2025 16:16	25/09/2025 19:08	2	1	9
266	16	25/09/2025 19:08	26/09/2025 22:08	4	2	1
267	17	26/09/2025 22:08	28/09/2025 01:07	5	4	2
268	18	28/09/2025 01:07	29/09/2025 03:54	6	5	4
269	19	29/09/2025 03:54	30/09/2025 06:17	7	6	5
270	20	30/09/2025 06:17	01/10/2025 08:06	8	7	6

Ser Nk	Date Entry	Date Exit	X Y Z
271 21	01/10/2025 08:06	02/10/2025 09:12	9 8 7
272 22	02/10/2025 09:12	03/10/2025 09:33	1 9 8
273 23	03/10/2025 09:33	04/10/2025 09:08	2 1 9
274 24	04/10/2025 09:08	05/10/2025 08:00	4 2 1
275 25	05/10/2025 08:00	06/10/2025 06:15	5 4 2
276 26	06/10/2025 06:15	07/10/2025 04:01	6 5 4
277 27	07/10/2025 04:01	08/10/2025 01:27	7 6 5
278 1	08/10/2025 01:27	08/10/2025 22:44	8 7 6
279 2	08/10/2025 22:44	09/10/2025 20:02	9 8 7
280 3	09/10/2025 20:02	10/10/2025 17:30	1 9 8
281 4	10/10/2025 17:30	11/10/2025 15:19	2 1 9
282 5	11/10/2025 15:19	12/10/2025 13:36	4 2 1
283 6	12/10/2025 13:36	13/10/2025 12:26	5 4 2
284 7	13/10/2025 12:26	14/10/2025 11:53	6 5 4
285 8	14/10/2025 11:53	15/10/2025 11:59	7 6 5
286 9	15/10/2025 11:59	16/10/2025 12:41	8 7 6
287 10	16/10/2025 12:41	17/10/2025 13:57	9 8 7
288 11	17/10/2025 13:57	18/10/2025 15:41	1 9 8
289 12	18/10/2025 15:41	19/10/2025 17:49	2 1 9
290 13	19/10/2025 17:49	20/10/2025 20:16	4 2 1
291 14	20/10/2025 20:16	21/10/2025 22:58	5 4 2
292 15	21/10/2025 22:58	23/10/2025 01:51	6 5 4
293 16	23/10/2025 01:51	24/10/2025 04:50	7 6 5
294 17	24/10/2025 04:50	25/10/2025 07:51	8 7 6
295 18	25/10/2025 07:51	26/10/2025 10:46	9 8 7
296 19	26/10/2025 10:46	27/10/2025 13:27	1 9 8
297 20	27/10/2025 13:27	28/10/2025 15:44	2 1 9
298 21	28/10/2025 15:44	29/10/2025 17:29	4 2 1
299 22	29/10/2025 17:29	30/10/2025 18:33	5 4 2
300 23	30/10/2025 18:33	31/10/2025 18:50	6 5 4

Ser	Nk	Date Entry	Date Exit	X	Y	Z
301	24	31/10/2025 18:50	01/11/2025 18:20	7	6	5
302	25	01/11/2025 18:20	02/11/2025 17:03	8	7	6
303	26	02/11/2025 17:03	03/11/2025 15:05	9	8	7
304	27	03/11/2025 15:05	04/11/2025 12:34	1	9	8
305	1	04/11/2025 12:34	05/11/2025 09:39	2	1	9
306	2	05/11/2025 09:39	06/11/2025 06:33	4	2	1
307	3	06/11/2025 06:33	07/11/2025 03:27	5	4	2
308	4	07/11/2025 03:27	08/11/2025 00:33	6	5	4
309	5	08/11/2025 00:33	08/11/2025 22:02	7	6	5
310	6	08/11/2025 22:02	09/11/2025 20:04	8	7	6
311	7	09/11/2025 20:04	10/11/2025 18:47	9	8	7
312	8	10/11/2025 18:47	11/11/2025 18:17	1	9	8
313	9	11/11/2025 18:17	12/11/2025 18:34	2	1	9
314	10	12/11/2025 18:34	13/11/2025 19:37	4	2	1
315	11	13/11/2025 19:37	14/11/2025 21:20	5	4	2
316	12	14/11/2025 21:20	15/11/2025 23:34	6	5	4
317	13	15/11/2025 23:34	17/11/2025 02:10	7	6	5
318	14	17/11/2025 02:10	18/11/2025 05:01	8	7	6
319	15	18/11/2025 05:01	19/11/2025 07:59	9	8	7
320	16	19/11/2025 07:59	20/11/2025 10:58	1	9	8
321	17	20/11/2025 10:58	21/11/2025 13:55	2	1	9
322	18	21/11/2025 13:55	22/11/2025 16:46	4	2	1
323	19	22/11/2025 16:46	23/11/2025 19:27	5	4	2
324	20	23/11/2025 19:27	24/11/2025 21:53	6	5	4
325	21	24/11/2025 21:53	25/11/2025 23:57	7	6	5
326	22	25/11/2025 23:57	27/11/2025 01:32	8	7	6
327	23	27/11/2025 01:32	28/11/2025 02:31	9	8	7
328	24	28/11/2025 02:31	29/11/2025 02:49	1	9	8
329	25	29/11/2025 02:49	30/11/2025 02:22	2	1	9
330	26	30/11/2025 02:22	01/12/2025 01:10	4	2	1

Ser	NK	Date Entry	Date Exit	X	Y	Z
331	27	01/12/2025 01:10	01/12/2025 23:17	5	4	2
332	1	01/12/2025 23:17	02/12/2025 20:51	6	5	4
333	2	02/12/2025 20:51	03/12/2025 17:59	7	6	5
334	3	03/12/2025 17:59	04/12/2025 14:53	8	7	6
335	4	04/12/2025 14:53	05/12/2025 11:45	9	8	7
336	5	05/12/2025 11:45	06/12/2025 08:48	1	9	8
337	6	06/12/2025 08:48	07/12/2025 06:13	2	1	9
338	7	07/12/2025 06:13	08/12/2025 04:11	4	2	1
339	8	08/12/2025 04:11	09/12/2025 02:52	5	4	2
340	9	09/12/2025 02:52	10/12/2025 02:22	6	5	4
341	10	10/12/2025 02:22	11/12/2025 02:43	7	6	5
342	11	11/12/2025 02:43	12/12/2025 03:55	8	7	6
343	12	12/12/2025 03:55	13/12/2025 05:49	9	8	7
344	13	13/12/2025 05:49	14/12/2025 08:18	1	9	8
345	14	14/12/2025 08:18	15/12/2025 11:08	2	1	9
346	15	15/12/2025 11:08	16/12/2025 14:09	4	2	1
347	16	16/12/2025 14:09	17/12/2025 17:11	5	4	2
348	17	17/12/2025 17:11	18/12/2025 20:06	6	5	4
349	18	18/12/2025 20:06	19/12/2025 22:50	7	6	5
350	19	19/12/2025 22:50	21/12/2025 01:21	8	7	6
351	20	21/12/2025 01:21	22/12/2025 03:35	9	8	7
352	21	22/12/2025 03:35	23/12/2025 05:32	1	9	8
353	22	23/12/2025 05:32	24/12/2025 07:07	2	1	9
354	23	24/12/2025 07:07	25/12/2025 08:18	4	2	1
355	24	25/12/2025 08:18	26/12/2025 09:00	5	4	2
356	25	26/12/2025 09:00	27/12/2025 09:09	6	5	4
357	26	27/12/2025 09:09	28/12/2025 08:42	7	6	5
358	27	28/12/2025 08:42	29/12/2025 07:40	8	7	6
359	1	29/12/2025 07:40	30/12/2025 06:03	9	8	7
360	2	30/12/2025 06:03	31/12/2025 03:57	1	9	8

361　3　31/12/2025 03:57　　　　　　2 1 9

Results of Moon Transit as Per Tara Bala

1. Mixed results with both auspicious and inauspicious events. An average day.
2. A good period bringing wealth, prosperity, enjoyment, and good fortune. Happiness in family.
3. A struggleful period with inauspicious results, crises, dangers, obstacles, and challenges on the material level.
4. Good results in terms of prosperity, wellbeing, and increased fortune. Overall prosperity, security, stability, and wellbeing.
5. Obstacles in all spheres of life, with obstructions, delays, and difficulties.
6. Achievements, accomplishments, successes, and fulfillment of goals. Achievement of desires through sincere efforts.
7. A struggle period with inauspicious results, obstacles, dangers, severe misfortunes, troubles, illness, or loss.
8. A good period with happiness, companionship, support from friends, gains through cooperation, and support.
9. Very good results with gains and highly auspicious events. Gains through friends, alliances, and overall positive outcomes.

Shani Sade sati and Remedies

Aries will come under the Shani Sade Sati, as Saturn transits to Pisces sign on 29 Mar 2025. When Saturn transits in the 12th, 1st and 2nd house of Moon Lagna or Janam Lagna, the individual is considered to be under the effect of Sadesati. Sadesati means 7 and a half years. "Sade Sati" is a term that creates fear in many people. It occurs approximately every 30 years in a person's life. In general, it is agreed that the Sadesati periods bring dissatisfaction, disappointment, depression, disagreements, disputes, disharmony, and undesirable outcomes. As a result, many individuals feel nervous about facing these challenges during such periods.

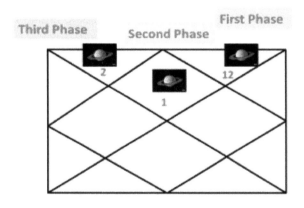

Sadesati comprises three Phases of 2.5 years each, known as "Dhaia," occurring when Saturn transits the 12th, 1st, or 2nd house for someone with a Moon sign as the Ascendant. The effects of all three phases are not necessarily negative for the individual directly. Instead, any indifferent or mixed results experienced indirectly may affect the individual, especially if they hold a position of authority or leadership within their household or institution.

Many people indeed experience positive events during the Sadesati period, such as promotions, business growth, marriages, childbirth, property acquisition, winning elections, purchasing new cars, and other successes. This contrasts with traditional interpretations, which often predict hardships, disappointments, disputes, and other negative outcomes during Sadesati.

The aspects of Saturn with other planets should also be considered, whether these aspects are favorable or unfavorable.

If Saturn is exalted, in its sign (Mool Trikona), in a friendly sign, or acting as a benefic or Yogakaraka (a planet that brings auspicious results).

When Saturn is strong in the birth chart but weak in transit, the results will be neutral. In such cases, there may not be significant loss or worries for the individual. Only when Saturn is weak in the birth chart and weak in transit can we presume malefic results.

So, I suggest rather than considering that Sade Sati for all individuals will result in problems, the factors mentioned above to be considered.

Effect of Sade Sati First Phase

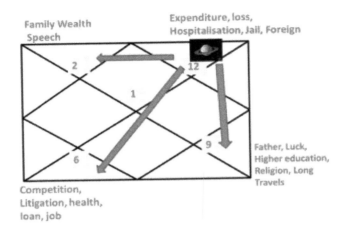

During the first phase of Sade Sati, when Saturn transits the 12th house of the horoscope for 2.5 years from 29 Mar 2025 onwards, the negative effects are primarily felt by the parents and close relatives of the individual. The Arians may find increase in expenditures, strained financial resources, loss of some family member, health issues, injury to legs, problems in foreign stay, loss of interest in sexual life. The individual may experience vision problems, possibly requiring the use of glasses, although major injuries or surgeries are unlikely except the period 7 June 2025 to 28 Jul 2025.

In the final period of Sade Sati's first phase, a person may feel compelled to embrace Sanyas, (Giving up worldly attachments) meaning they become detached from their family, wealth, home, and luxuries.

Remedies of Sade Sati

In case Aries people find major problems in their life due to Sade Sati, it is important to consider remedies to mitigate the negative impacts of Saturn. These remedies are beneficial in reducing the adverse effects.

You can choose one of the remedies or combine two or three of them to lessen Saturn's wrath when it is malefic in your chart.

Chanting of Mantras

Saturn's association with patience, slow actions and hard work gives it a natural inclination and ability to engage in repetitive chanting of mantras. Any of the mantras as under may be recited which matches your frequency.

- Om Sham Shanishwaraya Namah

- Om Pram Preem Proum Sah Shanishcharay Namah

- Om Suryaputra Dirghadeho Vishalakh Shivpraye

Mandchar Prassanatma Pida Haratu Me Shani
Nilaanjana-Samabhasam Ravi Putram Yamagrajam
Chayya-Martanda- Sambhutam Tam Namami Shanaishvaram

- Om Nilaanjana-Samabhasam Ravi Putram Yamagrajam

Chayya-Martanda- Sambhutam Tam Namami Shanaishvaram

- Om Tryambhakam yajamahe sugnadhim pushivardhan

Urvarukamiva bandhanan
mrityor moksheya mamratat Om

Gemstones

Each zodiac sign is associated with a planet and a gemstone, which can affect their lives according to their birth chart. Gemstones are considered to have a very effective influence over individuals. For Arians, I generally do not recommend Blue Sapphire as Saturn despite being lord of tenth and eleventh house is considered as malefic planet. There is no point in strengthening a malefic planet. However, If Saturn is not debilitated or in 8th or 12th houses then gem stone for Saturn can be tested during Sade sati period or when ever problem in professional matters arises.

Blue Sapphire is the main gemstone for Saturn. It should be worn in a ring with either gold or iron on the middle finger of the right hand for males and the left hand for females, specifically on Saturdays. The weight of the Sapphire should be at least 4 carats and free from flaws and defects.

Blue Sapphire is one the costly gemstones and everyone may not afford or do not want to risk investment without understanding the likely effect. In that case the cheaper options are to wear its substitutes. Substitutes are lapis lazuli, malachite or amethyst, which should be used in larger sizes (three to five carats) or as a pendant or strand.

All gemstones should be tested before wearing. Gems for Saturn should always be worn with care, as Saturn is a great malefic. Often it is best to give them a trial run, even if all factors appear good. They should not be used when there is too much darkness, selfishness, inertia, possessiveness, coldness, or calculation in nature - when the individual is proud or manipulative.

Other Practices

1. Visit the Shani temple on Saturdays. Offer mustard oil to Shani Idol on Saturdays.
2. Lord Shiva is the primary deity for Saturn, and all remedies for Saturn are dedicated to Lord Shiva. Whenever Trayodashi tithi and Saturday come together, it is the best time to do most of the remedies for Saturn including pujas, yagya or feeding for Shani. Shani was a devotee of Lord Shiva and Lord Shiva knows how to control the effects of Shani. Also, fasts for Saturn begin in the special month of Shravana and are dedicated to Lord Shiva.
3. Worship Lord Shiva on Mondays and observe a fast dedicated to them.
4. Wear Shani Yantra made of silver or copper as a pendant. This Yantra can also be kept in the Puja place at home after proper Puja (Pran Pratistha).
5. Wear the Rudraksha bead.
6. Avoid the dark blue colour of Saturn.
7. Helping poor and needy People is one of the best remedies to do for Saturn. You should feed the poor by donating food or helping the deprived people as a regular practice.
8. Avoid meat, alcohol, meat and eggs. Do not lie.

Afterword

Astrology is an enchanting subject that holds the secrets of our life's purpose. If we can understand even a part of it, we are considered fortunate. Each planet influences different aspects of human life, and some effects may go beyond our logical understanding. Learning more often makes us realize how much there is to explore, like taking a spoonful of water from an ocean of knowledge.

In this book, we have attempted to provide general predictions for this zodiac sign for the year 2025. We suggest taking these predictions as warnings to prepare yourself accordingly. We may not cover everything, as there is no limit to this field. Predicting events is a complex process because of the intricate connections between planets, signs, houses, Nakshatras, and their Padas. We rely on God's blessings and use our experience and knowledge to make predictions. However, the results may vary for each person depending on their natal chart, life phase, age, background, and location.

In the predictions for 2024, I have found a large number of events happened as predicted at different places. It reinforced our belief in the science of astrology. I encourage readers to share feedback on the insights discussed in this book so that we can all learn from each other's experiences. Together, we can discover more about the fascinating world of astrology and its impact on our lives.

Please remember wheel of time is always moving. Transit of planet in one Sign or another will continue. In an earthquake, weak houses get damaged. Houses having strong foundations and structures continue to stand tall even after a strong earthquake. Similarly, those who have strong motivation, character and relationships will stand past any transit with minor vibrations. Do not worry much about the transit but make yourself strong with hard work, dedication and good deeds.

God Bless You

Previous Predictions That become true

In my Annual Horoscope 2024, I have made some predictions that have proved true. Regarding Earthquakes, during Saturn Mars conjunction from 15 Mar to 23 Apr 2024 May 2025 - An earthquake of magnitude 7.4 occurred on 02 Apr 2024 16 km S of Hualien City event in Taiwan

Allegation over political parties and future of AAP and Kejriwal – A lot of politicians have been maligned and Arvind Kejriwal, President of AAP was arrested and put in jail for approx. 40 days. Fire incidents and accidents in May – June 2024, many such incidents have happened.

Regarding BJP victory in General Elections 2024- Despite the BJP slogan "400 Paar", my prediction regarding BJP is to work hard to form a government and take the support of others to prove the majority. BJP could get only 241 seats against the requirement of 272 so it will be forced to take the support of some parties to form government.

Ukraine-Russia issues remain unresolved. Ghaza, Palestine and rising support for Palestine, the world is witnessing increased support regarding that. Conversions are on the rise and the world is looking for this rise in a serious manner.

Gautam Institute of Vedic Astrology

Gautam Institute of Vedic Astrology (GIVA) has been established to enhance awareness of Vedic Astrology to those who have some interest in the subject. The purpose is to disseminate the knowledge and share it with the purpose of research and advancement of the subject. It is open to all who want to share their knowledge and those who want to learn through online classes, discussions, videos, and interactions.

Astrogiva.com,   @gautamdkastrologer   at   YouTube,   email: astrogautamdk@gmail.com

About the Authors

Dr Gautam DK, an engineer with, an MBA, MSc and Doctorate Degree in management, is from a family of Hindu Brahmins who have been engaged in astrology for centuries. Dr Gautam attended various courses as Jyotish Ratnakar, Jyotish Parveen, Jyotish Bhaskar, Jyotish Vibhushan, Jyotish Rishi, Nadi astrology, Palmistry, Vastu and Reiki Master. Now he is teaching Vedic astrology through his YouTube channel "Gautam DK Astrology" and website astrogiva.com and is involved in research on the subject. Email: astrogautamdk@gmail.com

————————————————————-—

Sh Naresh Gautam is the co-founder and the Chairman of GIVA. After his corporate career, he devoted himself to the field of astrology. He has been awarded the degree of Jyotish Ratan, Jyotish Bhushan, and Jyotish Prabhakar. He has been practicing astrology since the year 2000 and has a wide follower base all over the world. Due to his worldly experience, he provides very practical remedies for all the problems of life, which are not bound by fixed Karmas. Email: **nareshgautam2005@gmail.com**

Milton Keynes UK
Ingram Content Group UK Ltd.
UKHW021001211124
3007UKWH00031B/303